HEAT WAVE!

HEAT WAVE!

JANICE LAAKKO

atmosphere press

Published by Atmosphere Press

Cover design by Kevin Stone

Atmospherepress.com

*This book is dedicated to my daughter Karen
for her continuous support, and to the memory
of a very special student.*

CONTENTS

CHAPTER ONE

FORBIDDEN WOODS ADVENTURE

Dee entered her room and collapsed with fatigue on her bed. The transition to Lincoln Middle School was coming up in a few days, and she was feeling anxious about it. Her summer had been good for the most part, but thinking about returning to school was stressing her out. In elementary school, she had made three great friends: Sue, Ronnie, and Samantha. Would they all be together at Lincoln? Samantha had almost been left back, but she managed to squeak by, just barely. Dee took a deep breath and tried to relax. She was so sleepy...

Joey bounded into the room. "Wake up!" he said, as he tripped over sneakers that Dee had left in the middle of the floor.

"What?" Dee said, very groggy from her mini-nap.

"I have something to show you. It's the best thing ever! You won't believe it! But you have to come and see it for yourself!" Joey was always full of excitement and energy.

"Go away! I was sleeping! Leave me alone!" Dee pulled the covers over her head.

He pulled the covers off. "Don't be such a grouch! What I have to show you will definitely cheer you up—I promise. Please? I'll make your bed for a week if you come with me."

That was all it took for Dee to jump right out of bed and follow her brother to who knew where.

"One thing, though. You can't tell Mom or Dad. This is TOP SECRET!"

Dee raised her eyebrows. "Are you going to get us in trouble? Suddenly, I don't like the sound of this."

"No—I promise. But let's sneak out the back door."

Against her better judgment, she followed her brother. "Where are you taking me?" she asked. The route was closing in on a forbidden area. "We aren't going to the woods off Cosmer Street, are we? Mom and Dad said it's off-limits. Joey...?"

He didn't answer and kept walking. Finally, the destination was in full view, and it was, indeed, the forbidden area.

"You woke me up to bring me here? We're going to be grounded for life!" Dee was exasperated.

Joey made no comment and was now at a full jog, going into the woods.

Dee pleaded with him but to no avail. She couldn't leave him in the woods unattended, so she followed his lead, partly to make sure nothing bad happened to him and partly to satisfy her curiosity.

Deeper and deeper into the woods they went, with Dee's anxiety building at every step. It sure was creepy in there. They saw no one else.

Suddenly, there was movement under a pile of leaves.

Dee screamed, and out from under the leaves bolted a squirrel, likely terrified of her! "Let's go back!" she begged.

"No, what I want to show you is just behind this rock. Hurry!" Joey called with excitement.

When Dee rounded the bend, she stopped short and stared in amazement at the view in front of her. Behind the rock was a structure that looked like a metal closet. Joey went in, but Dee just peeked inside. There were lights flashing on what looked like a small desk. "What is this place?" she asked, but doubted that he knew any better than she.

"This is a real time machine!" Joey was bubbling over with enthusiasm. "Yesterday, I went back in time and saw you sit in some chocolate ice cream. Pete saw it, too! It was so funny, but the time machine sent me right back. I want to see if I can fix it so I can stay longer."

Dee was shocked. That event did actually happen, but she had never told Joey about it. Could this really be a time machine? Curiosity got the better of her, and she walked in.

"I'm going to try to send us into the future. I bet if I try this button..."

"Joey, DON'T!" But it was too late.

* * *

Dee found herself in an unfamiliar building. Her clothes felt tight. Very tight. And, she felt taller. Her mind felt foggy, as if in a haze. Where am I?

A pretty teenage girl approached her. "Can I help you? You look lost."

"I am lost. I was just with my brother, and I ended

up here." She turned around in search of Joey, but he was nowhere to be seen.

"I'm Penny. Are you, by any chance, Dee?"

"Yes, I am. How do you know me?"

"You were the only one who didn't show up for home-room, and I was sent out to look for you. Don't worry; the first day of high school is always scary. Every fresh-man gets lost. Anyway, as I said, I'm Penny. Each incom-ing ninth-grader is assigned a Big Sister or Big Brother for help and guidance. I'm your Big Sister. Nice to meet you, Dee."

High-school freshman? Last year, I was only in the fifth grade! *Dee was confused until she remembered the time machine.* If I'm here in high school, where did Joey end up? Is he in Lincoln Middle School in my place? *She shook her head in an attempt to clear her mind.*

"Nice to meet you too," she told Penny. "Have you seen my brother anywhere?"

"No, but we need to get you to homeroom."

Dee walked into the room and saw a few familiar faces, but they looked older somehow. She pulled at her clothes in an effort to alleviate the tightness, without any success. She took her schedule from the homeroom teacher and sat down.

English Grade 9? Geometry? Biology? World History? *She stopped reading and rubbed her head. It was all so overwhelming. She stood with the others for the Pledge of Allegiance.*

The bell rang, and she walked out with Penny at her side. They went together to Biology class. Penny was a kind girl, Dee noted, and she was happy that Penny had been chosen to be her Big Sister.

"I'll be back before the end of the period to help you get to the next class. It's going to be all right. You'll see."

"Thanks. I feel better, knowing that I have one ally in the building." Dee took a deep breath and walked into science class.

"Yes!" called a voice from across the room. "I was hoping we would be in classes together!" The young man approached Dee. "Hey, we made it to high school! Awesome to see you!"

Dee couldn't help but smile when she realized that the handsome boy was none other than Pete Hawkins, her friend from elementary school. "Middle school seemed to go by in a blink," she quipped.

Pete went on to tease her about some of the class adventures they had experienced in middle school, but Dee couldn't recall ever being there.

The teacher asked for the students' attention so that he could explain what they were expected to learn in the next ten months. And so it went for the rest of the day. Dee was in Biology with Pete, English with Sue, and Geometry with Ronnie. However, Samantha was not in any of her classes.

She called Samantha after school. "Hi, it's me! How was your first day of school?"

Samantha began to sob. "I don't know. I'm lost on the first day of math. We were working on algebra, and I didn't know any of it. My Big Sister, Anya, couldn't help me either."

Dee offered some encouragement and said that she'd check in tomorrow.

* * *

"Penny! I'm so happy to see you!" Dee exclaimed as she walked into school the next day. "Thanks for helping me yesterday. I was a nervous wreck!"

"First-day jitters are normal. I'm glad I could help."

"I think I can find my classes okay today, but I have a favor to ask you."

Penny smiled. "What do you need, Little Sister?"

"I don't need help, but my friend Samantha does. She's already having trouble in math. Are you good at algebra?"

"Am I good in math? Yes, I love it!"

"Could you come over to my house this afternoon and meet Samantha?" Dee asked hopefully.

"I'd love to meet her and help her with math." Penny was truly the best Big Sister in the high school.

The afternoon went great, and Samantha left feeling much better. Dee slept well that night, knowing that she had the best friends in the whole world.

CHAPTER TWO

LAST DAYS OF SUMMER

"Dee, wake up!"

She awoke with a start, as Joey yelped after tripping over her sneakers.

"What's the matter?" Dee sat upright in bed, wondering what the fuss was about.

"You never answered us, so Mom sent me up here to get you for supper. Are you sick?"

"No, I'm not sick. In fact, I'm delighted that you'll be making my bed for a week. And I know your secret: that you go to the woods off Cosmer Street. That should get me out of doing dishes for the rest of my life!"

"What are you talking about? We aren't allowed to go there. Stop trying to think of ways to get me in trouble!"

Dee got up and grabbed Joey by the shoulder. "I know about the time machine," she whispered.

Joey ran out of the room. "MOM!"

Shortly thereafter, Mrs. Lanson came in with a thermometer in her hand. "I think we had better take your temperature. You don't look well."

"I feel fine," Dee said. "High school isn't so bad. I really like my Big Sister, Penny. She is SO nice." Suddenly, she felt dizzy and eased herself back onto the bed.

Mrs. Lanson checked the thermometer. "You have a high fever, so you'll have to stay in bed. Middle school starts soon, and you'll need to be well for that."

Dee sulked. "You mean I was *never* in high school?"

"I'm sorry to tell you this, but you've been in your bed all afternoon. I'll get you some medication and liquids to help with this fever."

When Mrs. Lanson returned, she found Dee wiping tears from her eyes. "What's wrong?"

"I met this really awesome girl named Penny at high school. She was so nice to me, and she even helped Samantha. She was smart, too. Now I know it was all just a dream. A stupid dream. And Penny isn't even real!" A stray tear dripped onto the bed.

"Did you say Penny?" Mrs. Lanson asked with wonder.

"Yes, why?" Dee said as she grabbed a tissue to dry her face.

"Samantha's mother just hired a high-school student to help Samantha with math once school starts. Her name is Penny. Maybe you heard me mention her name when I was talking to Samantha's mother."

Dee brightened up. *Could this be the Penny from my dream?* Suddenly, she couldn't wait for school to begin!

* * *

Dee's enthusiasm plummeted as her illness persisted. She had planned on visiting the middle school prior to the first day so that she could learn the layout of the building. Fear gripped her as she imagined being unable to find the locations of her classes. Too sick to do anything about it, she could only just lie there and worry.

The one bright thought was meeting Penny. Dee was eager to see if she was the girl from her dream.

Joey knocked on her bedroom door. "Hey, Dee," he called from the doorway. "I was going to ask if you wanted to play a game. Mom said no because she doesn't want me to get sick, but I can talk to you from here."

Normally, Dee would have told him to get lost, but she was lonely, so she agreed. "So, if you could really travel through time, where would you go and when?"

Joey sat, looking thoughtful. "Maybe I'd go back to when the Pilgrims came to America. Then I could meet a real Native American and be at the first Thanksgiving. That'd be cool. I'd eat all the turkey!"

"Samantha did a project on Native Americans last year. Meeting the Pilgrims would be cool, but I think I'd like to go back in time to see what Mom and Dad were like when they were our age," Dee said.

Joey laughed. "Do you think Dad was a nerd? He's really smart. I bet he was wicked nerdy."

"Mom's smart, too," Dee reminded him. "I don't think she would act nerdy, though. I wonder if she was nervous like me."

"You know where a cool place to go would be?" Joey said.

"Joey, there's a call for you," Mrs. Lanson called from the hall. He scrambled to his feet and was gone. Dee would be left to wonder what he was going to say.

She felt better with each passing day. The day before school began, she felt almost back to normal.

"Dee! Phone!" Joey walked into her room, a portable phone in his hand.

"Hello?" Dee said quietly.

"Hey, it's Sue. I'm wondering if you'd like to come over after school tomorrow."

"I'll check with Mom, but I bet it'll be okay. Did you check out the school? I was going to, but didn't get to do it."

"Yeah, I went yesterday. I called you, but your mom said you weren't up to it. Don't worry; it'll be easy to find your way around. You'll see."

Dee felt better about that, finally.

"I'm excited!" Sue said. "Can you believe it—we're going to middle school!"

"I'm nervous, but a little excited too."

"Dee!" Mrs. Lanson called. "Time for dinner!"

"Got to go. See you tomorrow!" Dee clicked the phone off and joined her family.

Joey was ecstatic about school. He would finally get to be in Advance, the program for gifted students. He was chatting away excitedly between bites of supper.

"You'll like Advance," Dee said. "You'll do some creative projects. The teachers are nice, too."

"I'll be even better at it than you were." Joey stuffed some potatoes into his mouth.

"That's enough of that kind of talk," Mrs. Lanson declared. "There will be no comparing."

Dee glared at him. "Hey, maybe you could do a special project on the germs living in your desk. Last year you brought home a bag of stuff from school—and there was old food in there! There must've been tons of germs...."

"Kids! That is quite enough! Let's keep the mealtime pleasant," Mrs. Lanson said emphatically.

Dee pouted. She always seemed to get spoken to more sharply than Joey did. At least, that was how she felt about it.

Mr. Lanson was notably silent during the heated exchanges.

"Joe, is everything all right? You haven't said a word," Mrs. Lanson asked with a concerned tone. He appeared sad and uninterested, which was different from his usual happy and encouraging demeanor.

"I'm sorry. I guess I have a lot on my mind." Turning to Dee and Joey, he said, "Tomorrow you will begin a new school year. Be good and study hard, and you'll be off to a great start."

"I'm always good, and I always study hard," Dee said with a smile.

Joey burst out laughing, with bits of food spewing out of his mouth onto the table in front of him.

"Ew! You are *so* gross!" Dee screeched.

Mrs. Lanson was tired of the bickering and simply announced that suppertime was over. She was more concerned about her husband than the sibling squabble. He was definitely not acting like himself.

Dee left the table to gather her school supplies and choose her clothes. Her nervousness was replaced with excitement. She was going to middle school!

CHAPTER THREE

TOO MANY SURPRISES

The first day of school had arrived, with pelting rain beating against the windowpanes. *Is this an omen of unpleasant things to come?* Dee wondered about such things.

Something she noticed about Lincoln Middle School was the noise. Kids were laughing and talking with one another using their outdoor voices. There was a fair amount of pushing and shoving. A boy went running by Dee and nearly knocked her over. That didn't help her nervousness one bit. Teachers were trying to keep order, but it was clearly not working.

Because of large groups of students hanging out in the halls, Dee couldn't see the room numbers. She looked at the schedule she had received in the mail. Room 20 was her homeroom.

Sue approached her from behind. "Hey ya!" she said enthusiastically.

Dee turned around and was relieved to see a friendly face. "I can't find my homeroom," she said quietly. "Do you know where Room 20 is?" She felt as though a family of butterflies had taken up residence in her stomach.

"It's right next to mine. Follow me!" Sue led the way, and Dee walked behind, grateful for this stroke of good luck.

There were so many new faces in homeroom. She recognized very few. Feeling awkward, she wished that she had the courage to join in on some of the conversations. Everyone else seemed to be having a lot more fun than she was. No one came over to meet her, so she sat alone, miserable.

Her subjects were in different classrooms, and from the look of her schedule, the rooms were spread out around the school. Her first class was Math, located in Room 2.

She headed out when the bell rang to find the class, but with so many students in the hall, she still had trouble finding the room numbers. She walked around the school but couldn't seem to find the correct room.

Finally, she saw an older boy standing against the wall. He looked friendly. She guessed that he was positioned there to help new students find their way.

"Could you tell me where Room 2 is?" Dee managed to ask.

"Sure," the boy said with a wide smile. "Turn around, go straight down the hall, and turn left. Go to the end of that hall, and Room 2 will be on your right."

"Thanks!" Dee said, relieved that she would finally get to class. She followed the directions perfectly, but ended up at the gym!

That loser! He sent me to the gym, and I thought he

was nice! Dee was now stressed because the second bell had just rung, and she was not in class. She tried not to panic, but she was lost and unsure what to do next.

"Can I help you find your way?"

Dee looked up and saw a man who might be a teacher. She took a deep breath and said, "I'm lost and late for class." A tear escaped from her eye.

"I'm Mr. Collins, one of the gym teachers. This must be your first day at this school." Dee nodded. "May I see your schedule?" She handed him the schedule. "What grade are you in?"

"Sixth grade," Dee said.

"All sixth-grade classes are held in the wing labeled A. That's on the other side of the building. I'll bring you there. Follow me."

Dee was embarrassed that she had gotten lost and needed to be walked to class, but the boy in the hall had lied to her and sent her to the gym. *Not my fault.*

Upon arriving to class, she thanked Mr. Collins and walked in. She was afraid that she'd get in trouble, but that would be the least of her problems. She looked at the teacher and stopped dead in her tracks. *No! It can't be!* For standing in the front of the room was none other than Ms. Hersh, the teacher of dread from her elementary school!

"Delores, please come in and join us," Ms. Hersh said. The only vacant seat was right in the front, next to the teacher's desk. Dee sat down.

"As I was telling the class, last year I taught fifth grade at North Elementary, and now I have moved on to the sixth grade, just like all of you. Some of you have had me as your teacher before." She flashed a smile at Dee. "I am tough and strict, but you *will* learn math."

Some of the students started talking while Ms. Hersh was explaining what they would be studying. Dee knew what was going to happen next.

"THAT WILL BE ENOUGH OF THAT!" Ms. Hersh shouted. "When I am speaking, you WILL be silent." She took down the names of the disrupters and put their names on the board. It became so quiet, one could hear a pin drop.

"I am a baseball fan," she said once everyone had settled. "Strike one: your name goes on the board. Strike two: you get extra homework problems. Strike three: you are out! Out of the room, and your parents are called. Do you understand the rules?"

"Yes, Ms. Hersh, but what if there's a strike four?" Dee recognized the voice: *Andrew Burke.* Andrew was a troublemaker in elementary school. Dee was one of his favorite targets to tease. He also got in quite a bit of trouble with Ms. Hersh.

Ms. Hersh turned and gave him the look that was all too familiar to her former students. Her eyes, under the deep lines of her forehead, would become like slits, while all the muscles in her face would become tense. She would raise her head and look down at the poor offending student below.

The class dared not move. "I do not recommend that anyone reach strike four. Thank you for your question, Andrew."

Order was restored, the lesson began, and homework was assigned. The bell rang, which ended the period.

Dee looked at her schedule and saw that her next class was in Room 15. Mr. Collins had mentioned that all the sixth-grade rooms were in A-wing, right where she was, but she thought she had seen Room 15 in another hall.

When she entered the hall, the crowd once again blocked her view of the room numbers, so she trusted her instinct and went to the other wing.

Just then there was a loud, piercing noise—the fire alarm was going off! Startled, she looked around for familiar faces but saw no one she recognized. She covered her ears and followed the crowd outside. Most of the students there looked older, so she had guessed wrong, again. Room 15 must have been in A-wing after all.

She stood nervously, waiting for the students to be let back into the building. The alarm continued to blare, annoying her. It was at least 15 minutes before students could reenter the building, and although the heavy rain had let up, it was still drizzling. The whole experience was unnerving! Finally, the students were allowed to return to class, and Dee found her way back to A-wing and the elusive Room 15.

Dee went over to Sue's house after school. Dee told her about Ms. Hersh, and Sue was quite surprised to hear the news. Sue had not seen Ms. Hersh, a fact she was very happy about! Sue put on some music, and she and Dee chatted, and after a while Dee announced that she should go home. She was quite tired from her first day and wanted some alone time.

At home, Dee reflected on the day. Because the graduates from all local elementary schools attended Lincoln, the classes were all mixed. Dee had hoped all her friends would be in every class with her, but that didn't prove to be the case. She had at least one class with each of her friends; the one unlucky part was having three classes with Andrew, the fifth-grade nuisance.

Dee then realized that she had gone the entire day without seeing Pete. Maybe he was absent.

Pete had been her rival in elementary school. Both were very intelligent and in Advance. Dee couldn't understand her feelings. *If he's my rival, why do I care where he is?* Friendship. Pete was nice to Dee—unlike Andrew.

Well, she had made it through her first day as a sixth-grader. It hadn't been easy, and at times, it hadn't been fun. Tomorrow would be better. Wouldn't it?

CHAPTER FOUR

LIAR, LIAR, JUMP IN THE FIRE

The following day, there was still no sign of Pete. At lunchtime, as if reading her mind, Andrew approached her. "Looking for someone?" he asked with a smirk on his face.

"Not you," Dee said, and she turned her face away from him.

"If you're looking for Pete, he isn't here."

"I wasn't," Dee lied. "Is he sick?"

"No, but he won't be back. He goes to some fancy school now."

Dee's heart sank. "How come?"

"Beats me. Hey—what's this? Do you LIKE him?" With that, he ran back to his table of friends, chanting, "Dee likes Pete; Dee likes Pete!"

Dee turned red. "Jerk!" she muttered under her breath.

"Hey, what's up, Dee?" Sue asked as she sat down at the table. "You look mad."

"Andrew, that's what. He's such a jerk! And he's in three of my classes. This year's going to stink!"

Samantha joined the group late. "Dee, can you come over later today? Penny's coming to help with math, but after that would be good. You could stay for dinner if you want. Mom said you could."

A lightbulb went off in Dee's mind. *Perfect.*

"Yeah. I don't think Mom will mind. What time?"

"After 4:00?" Samantha said. "Tutoring ends at 4:00."

"Okay," Dee agreed, excited about their plan. Today, she would find out if Penny was the girl from her dream.

Upon arriving home, Dee received permission to go to Samantha's but had to tell a tiny lie to do so. Mrs. Lanson knew about the tutoring session because she had spoken to Samantha's mother earlier in the day. When Mrs. Lanson heard the time from Dee—3:30—she said no. Dee whined and then said that the tutoring session had been canceled because Penny was sick. Mrs. Lanson finally agreed.

Dee walked into Samantha's house at 3:35. Mrs. Perry looked surprised to see her and directed her to the living room.

"Samantha is working with Penny until 4:00. I'm sorry. Samantha must have told you the wrong time."

"No, she didn't. She said 4:00." *How am I going to get out of this one?* "This was the only time Mom could drive me." *Uh-oh—two lies—not good!* "I don't mind waiting."

Dee was nervous and excited. At 4:02, she jumped up and ran into the hall when she heard Samantha saying goodbye to Penny. "Hi!" she said awkwardly.

Penny, whose back was toward Dee, turned around. Dee stood speechless—her mouth open in awe. This was, indeed, the Penny from her dream!

"Hi, Dee," Penny said. "Nice to see you again."

"You know me?" Dee managed to say.

"Of course! Don't you remember? I met you a while ago at a community picnic. I was asked to help with the younger kids. You and Joey were in that group."

"Oh, yeah," Dee fibbed. She didn't remember meeting Penny at the picnic, but she must have; how else would she have been able to dream about her? So, Dee now knew the truth, although it had taken lying to satisfy her curiosity.

The two friends sat together on the living-room floor. "You look mad or something. What's wrong?" Samantha asked.

"Well, I *am* mad. I was just thinking about school today. Why do I have to be in classes with Andrew? He's so mean! He bugs me, and I can't stand him!"

"Is he worse this year?" Samantha asked with a puzzled look on her face.

"You should've seen what he did to me in the cafeteria. He's so annoying!" Dee proceeded to describe the incident in full detail.

"Whoa. Do you think Pete really went to another school?"

"Well, if he did, I bet he did it to get away from Andrew!"

Samantha smiled mischievously. "Maybe we should all join Pete and leave Andrew alone with Ms. Hersh!"

The girls laughed very hard at that thought.

Samantha changed the subject and brought up Penny. "This was our first tutoring session, and she helped me a lot. I understand the math now. She's so nice, too."

"I wonder if she could help me with my problem at

school—getting rid of Andrew! I'd like to have tutoring in that!" Dee exclaimed.

The conversation came to an end when Samantha's mother called them to the supper table.

* * *

Once at home, Dee settled in to do her homework. As she was working on a math assignment, her parents entered the room. *Uh-oh.*

"Dee, could we speak to you a minute?" Mrs. Lanson asked. It wasn't really a question, as Dee well knew.

"Your mother has mentioned a couple of disturbing things," Mr. Lanson added. "We would like an explanation."

Dee swallowed hard and waited. She went over in her mind all the things that she could be in trouble for and which of those things her parents had become aware of.

"Mrs. Perry told me that you arrived at their home in the middle of Samantha's tutoring session. You told me that Penny was sick and canceled the lesson," Mrs. Lanson said. "Can you explain this?"

"Sorry, Mom," Dee said quietly.

"As I heard it, you then told Mrs. Perry that 3:30 was the only time your mother could drive you," Mr. Lanson added.

"Two lies, Dee. You have been brought up to be honest. Lying is never the right thing to do. What were you thinking?" Mrs. Lanson asked.

Dee squirmed in her seat and looked down at the floor. "I wanted to see if Penny was the girl from my dream. The only way I could find out was to go over there. Then Mrs.

Perry sounded like she was going to blame Samantha, so I made up that Mom could only drive me then." Dee avoided eye contact with her parents. "I'm sorry," she muttered.

"Lying to us is unacceptable. You're grounded for two days. No friends, and no phone calls or email," Mrs. Lanson said. She and Mr. Lanson promptly left the room.

Although Dee thought the punishment was a bit harsh, she dared not say so to her parents. She went back to her homework but had a hard time focusing on it. Middle-school life was challenging!

CHAPTER FIVE

REALLY, RONNIE?

"Has anyone seen Ronnie lately?" Samantha asked Dee and Sue the next day during lunch.

"She's in my History class," Dee offered, "but she doesn't really talk to me. She talks to two girls from South Elementary. When I look for her after class, I can't find her. I haven't seen her at lunch, either."

"I called her house last night, but she was too busy to come to the phone," Sue said. "Why don't we plan to hang out at my house after school and ask Ronnie to come?"

Dee didn't want her friends to know that she was grounded for lying to her parents, so she made up an excuse. "I can't. I have to go to the dentist." *Oops! Another lie.*

"Didn't you just go to the dentist?" Samantha asked.

"Well, my dentist is *really* careful." Dee was feeling cornered and didn't like it one bit. She hated lying. It always brought more trouble than the trouble she was trying to avoid. Yet, to get out of a jam, she did it anyway.

All of a sudden, someone approached the table and sat next to Dee. It was Andrew. He made kissing noises at her. "Are you missing Pete?" he jeered. His question was followed by more kissing noises and hysterical laughter.

"Get lost! Stop BOTHERING me!" Dee was seriously angry now. Andrew took the hint and left—but not without first blowing her a kiss.

"Whoa," Samantha said. "You weren't kidding about Andrew. What a pain. Why's he bugging you?"

Dee shook her head. "Who knows?"

The bell rang; lunch was over. "Bye, everyone," Sue said. "Good luck at the dentist, Dee."

Math followed lunch, and Dee avoided even looking at Andrew. He didn't bother her, likely because Ms. Hersh was in the room. Suddenly, Dee realized that having Ms. Hersh for a teacher might be a very good thing—at least where Andrew was concerned.

Ms. Hersh made an announcement at the end of the period. "I would like you to buy a specific calculator for this class. It is called a graphing calculator. If you buy the one I recommend, then you can use it all through high school." She proceeded to give the information so that the students would know which calculator to buy. "It is expensive, but will be worth it."

Dee was waiting for Andrew to come out with a wisecrack, but he remained silent. When class was over, the students ran for the door. Another student, named Nolan, pushed Andrew right into Dee.

"Hey, watch out!" Andrew called.

"Why don't you watch out yourself!" came the reply.

Even though Nolan was bigger, Andrew ran after him

and gave him a shove. Then it happened. The two boys got into a fight, right there in the hallway! Others gathered around to see who would win the battle.

Nolan threw the first punch, and Andrew ducked under it. Andrew pushed Nolan into the crowd, and he stumbled but didn't fall. Nolan then went to hit Andrew in the face, but Andrew put his arms up to block it and got one arm scratched in the process. Before the winner could be declared, Ms. Hersh broke through the crowd.

"ENOUGH!" she yelled. "Both of you to the principal's office. NOW!"

Andrew looked like he had gotten the worst of it. His arm was bleeding a little, and his face was red. Dee felt a bit sorry for him. Just a tiny bit. He had been shoved into her, which started the whole debacle. This was one case where Andrew was not to blame for starting something.

The rest of the school day held no real surprises. Dee went home and faced her punishment—isolation from her friends.

She wondered what was going on with Ronnie. She seemed to be avoiding everyone. *Have we done something wrong?* Dee tried to remember their last conversation but could not. She hoped this didn't mean the beginning of the end for the once Fantastic Four!

* * *

It was Friday, finally. Dee looked back over the week and pondered all that had taken place. She had had a rocky start to middle school.

For one thing, she had been sent on a wild goose chase while trying to find her class. The seemingly nice boy in the hall turned out to be a mischief-maker. Stern Ms. Hersh was back as her teacher. There was a fire drill on the first day of school. The first day! Dee had lied so that she could see Penny and got grounded for it. Andrew was being a pain already. She had found out that Pete was going to a different school. The most puzzling thing of all was the situation with Ronnie. Dee decided that she would get to the bottom of it.

Over the past couple of days, she had become increasingly comfortable at school. She had learned her way around the building and settled into all her classes. Her mother had taken her and Joey out shopping for school supplies, including the calculator, so she was all set. Working with a calculator that she would still use in high school made her proud. She might even enjoy having Ms. Hersh for a teacher—although she couldn't quite imagine it.

History was her second class. She would try to talk to Ronnie.

Dee hurried to arrive early, but the crowd in the hall delayed her. By the time she got to class, Ronnie was surrounded by three other girls, and she never even looked over at Dee. Ronnie was laughing and flipping her long red hair back in a manner that Dee thought was conceited.

What's happening to Ronnie? She acts so differently. She acts like she thinks she's better than everyone. Dee approached the group but lost her nerve, went to her seat, and sat down.

Mr. Chu called the class to order. "We will be studying some of our early Presidents. I'm going to divide the class into groups. Each group will research a President and then make a presentation to the class." He read the names for Group One, who would research George Washington. "Group Two will be Brenda Jackson, Ronnie McCormick, Delores Lanson, and..." Mr. Chu paused and looked through the class list.

Perfect! Dee thought. *Now I can see if there's a problem with Ronnie.*

"And," Mr. Chu continued, "Andrew Burke."

No! It can't be! Dee's lightened mood suddenly darkened. She heard nothing else Mr. Chu said after that. Her mind was racing with all kinds of thoughts.

The students separated into their groups and awaited their assignment. Dee tried to sit next to Ronnie, but Brenda grabbed the chair just as Dee was reaching for it. Dee noticed that Brenda was one of the girls Ronnie had been talking to before class.

Dee took the remaining seat, next to Andrew and across from Brenda. "Hey, Ronnie," she said.

Ronnie glanced over and said a quiet and unenthusiastic, "Hey." She and Brenda then talked among themselves, totally ignoring Dee.

Dee sulked in her seat.

Andrew leaned over and whispered, "I talked to Pete last night. Jealous?"

"No, I am not jealous," Dee replied. This was another lie, because she did miss Pete, especially because Ronnie was being difficult and Andrew was such a pest. Pete had been her rival, but trying to do better than he did on tests had made her an even better student.

Andrew was about to say more, but was interrupted by Mr. Chu. "Your group will research President John Adams."

President Adams? Dee didn't know anything about the man, but she did like projects. Group work was not her favorite, though, because group members often didn't do their part. She hoped that this group would be a good one.

Dee, being quiet, hoped someone would get the conversation started about the project. There was planning that had to be done so that each student would know what to do. However, Brenda and Ronnie continued to talk to each other in quiet voices. Dee noticed that Ronnie was sitting up extra straight and repeatedly flipping her hair in that conceited way. Andrew was rubbing the scratch he had on his arm from the fight. No one was focused on the History project.

"Does anyone have any ideas for the project?" Dee finally asked.

Ronnie and Brenda didn't answer. It was Andrew who spoke up. "Nope, not a one. I got nuthin'."

"The project is due next Friday," Dee reminded the group. "Why don't we each take a part to research?"

"Whatever," Ronnie said. "I don't care what I do."

"Me neither," said Brenda.

"Ditto," came the third response.

Dee knew that she would have to take matters into her own hands. "How about we divide the topic up into four parts? One part could be his early life. Another could be what he was like as a President. Any other ideas?"

"Nope." The response was a perfect chorus.

Dee didn't know anything about any of the Presidents, except for George Washington, so she wasn't sure what else they should include. "Forget it. Why don't we all do our own research over the weekend? We can figure out what to do for the presentation next week."

"Whatever," Ronnie said.

Ronnie was really getting on Dee's nerves. She was not

the nice friend who was part of the Fantastic Four.

The bell rang. Class was over, and their group had accomplished nothing. Dee resolved that she would work hard over the weekend. She wanted an A on the project!

CHAPTER SIX

WORST GROUP IN THE WORLD

Over the weekend, Dee worked for hours on her History project. She had written four pages of facts about President John Adams. She hoped that the others had worked as hard on it, because the group had to give a presentation on Friday. History was last period on Monday.

Dee wasn't certain that she liked the rotating schedule. No one class met at the same time each day; the classes were on a five-day rotation. It gave Dee the feeling that the days were all mixed up. However, one advantage of History being last today was that, maybe, she could ask Ronnie to come over after school and work on the project.

History class began, and the time was dedicated to the project. Students were discussing their presentations in every group but one: Dee's group. The lack of focus was annoying Dee, so once again, she spoke up.

"I wrote four pages of notes." She proceeded to take them out of her desk. No one else made any move. "What did you guys do?"

"I didn't get to it," Brenda said.

"Neither did I," Ronnie added with a giggle and a hair flip.

"Get to what?" Andrew flashed a mischievous smile at Dee.

"The project, that's what!" Dee was infuriated. "I did all this work, and you all did *nothing*?"

"I'll just copy yours," Andrew said as he reached across the desk to snag Dee's notes.

Quicker than a cheetah, Dee pulled the papers right out from under him. "That's cheating. I'm going to tell Mr. Chu what you said."

"Tell me what?" Mr. Chu inquired. He had been standing by their group and had escaped everyone's notice.

No one said anything, including Dee. She didn't want to get in trouble because she wanted a good grade on the project.

"Friday will be here before you know it," Mr. Chu reminded them. "It is best not to leave everything until the last minute. Try to work on the project each day. Then it won't seem like such a big deal."

Resentment was building up inside Dee. She expected this sort of laziness from Andrew, but not from Ronnie.

The rest of the class period was unproductive, but she had an idea. She decided to ask Ronnie over after school anyway. The dismissal bell rang, and Dee hurried to catch up to her sprinting friend.

"Hey, wait up!" Dee called loudly.

Ronnie did slow down, but when she turned in Dee's direction, Dee thought she detected an eye-roll. "What?"

"Well, I guess you were busy this weekend, so I thought

we could get together at my house and work on the project. Can you come over?"

"No, I'm busy," Ronnie said impatiently. "Gotta go. I don't want to miss my bus." And, she was off.

Dee considered her options. She didn't know Brenda at all, and asking Andrew over was out of the question. At the moment, she had her own bus to catch.

At home, Dee decided that she would ask her parents what to do about this new problem. She would ask them at supper. In the meantime, she worked on her math homework, which she finished very quickly.

Playing with her new calculator proved to be a good distraction. She pushed all kinds of buttons and had no idea what many of them meant. It was called a graphing calculator, but after trying several buttons, she saw no graphs show up on the screen. Maybe she would have to wait for high school to learn how to work all the features.

Joey ran in to tell Dee that it was time to eat. She appeared eagerly, hoping to get help with her problem.

Mr. Lanson was sitting at the table and seemed glum. He appeared to be thinking hard about something.

"Hey, Dad," Dee said. "How was your day?"

"I would rather hear about yours," he said.

Dee blurted out the whole History project problem and waited for some wise words of advice from him.

"That's a tough one, Dee. What do you think you should do about it?"

"I don't know. That's why I'm asking you!"

"Just ask your teacher," Mr. Lanson said sharply.

Everyone froze in place; this was not an expected response. Dee depended on her parents to help her with the big problems. She started to cry. "Dad..." she whined.

"Joe, is everything all right?" Mrs. Lanson asked.

He sighed. "We'll talk later." Turning to Dee, he said, "I'm sorry. I didn't mean to upset you. I just think your teacher is the best one to help with a problem involving classmates."

Since when? Dee was confused about her father's peculiar behavior of late. She wiped her eyes and tried to eat. Trying to hold back tears made her choke on her food.

"Stop coughing!" Joey exclaimed.

With that, Dee got up from the table and ran to her room. She expected that, in time, her parents would follow. Maybe they would feel bad and offer to help. Maybe they would at least give her a few ideas for what to do. She waited, but nobody came.

* * *

Each day brings a ray of hope that the new day will be better than the one before. These were wise words from her once-helpful parents. Dee was determined to solve her problems, by herself if she had to. She had so many problems at the moment, but the most pressing one was the project. *I will find a way to fix this!*

History was the third class, right before lunch. Go figure. *Does mixing up classes every day make any sense?* Dee didn't think so. But she had no choice in the matter, so she just went along with it. She entered the class with a degree of hope that somebody would have done something.

The class broke up into their groups, and Mr. Chu passed out a mini-laptop computer to each student. He gave some brief instructions on how to access the Internet and told the students to ask if they had any trouble.

"So, what did you guys do on the project?" Dee asked hopefully.

"I didn't have time to do anything. I was busy, like I told you yesterday." Ronnie looked at Dee icily.

"I didn't have time to do anything either," Brenda offered.

"That's what I was supposed to do!" said Andrew. "I knew I had to do something for homework, but I forgot what it was!"

This is THE WORST group in the world! Dee felt panicked. She didn't know what to do. *Should I tell Mr. Chu what's going on, that they're not doing any work?* Surely that would get the others in trouble, but then they would be mad at her for squealing. That would lead to even more problems at school. The year had just begun. She didn't want to start accumulating enemies. Maybe the computers would help.

Ronnie and Brenda were writing something down as they looked at the computer. Dee was hopeful and worked on her own project, not daring to ask any of them about their progress. She felt that her part of the project was good and hoped the others would get their acts together and do a good job, too.

"What shall we do for a presentation?" she asked cautiously.

"I don't know," Ronnie said flatly. "You could present for our group what you've done."

Dee was stunned. Of all people to pass the responsibility onto someone else! Ronnie had become someone Dee no longer knew.

The others seemed to think Ronnie's idea was a good

one. *Of course.* Dee hated to admit it, but even she could see some benefit to being the presenter—although she was quite annoyed by the reason. However, it just might be the only way they could get a good grade.

Friday came, and Dee's group was to present second because John Adams was the second President. The first group had done a good job. Each student had contributed to the presentation. Dee didn't know what the others in her group were going to do if they were called upon. She had been afraid to ask them.

Mr. Chu said, "Very nicely presented. Group Two, please give your presentation on our second President, John Adams."

Dee stood up and presented her research. She had a couple of pictures to show that she had downloaded off the Internet. She felt confident about her presentation and returned to her seat.

"Thank you," said Mr. Chu. "Now, let's hear from the others in your group."

Ronnie started to read something, but Mr. Chu interrupted her. "Ronnie, you appeared to research the wrong President. Please return to your seat."

Brenda had nothing written down and tried to restate facts that Dee had mentioned in her presentation, but that went no better. Brenda mixed up all the facts, so her presentation made no sense. Dee's hope was on Andrew to save the day.

"Well," began Andrew, "I think a company named their beer after him."

The class roared in laughter. "What?" he said in a confused tone.

"Samuel Adams does not equal John Adams," Mr. Chu

told him, "and I will not ask how you know about such things. Your group did not follow the guidelines for the project, and this will be reflected in your grade. Let's hear from the next group."

Dee was furious. *How could they do this to me?* Unable to focus on the other presentations, she just sat and sulked.

At the end of the class period, each group received its grade for the presentation. Mr. Chu began, "Among the six groups, there were two A's, three B's, and one D. The grade was based mostly on how well members within the group worked together..."

Well, there it was. Dee knew immediately which group had scored the lowest. She was devastated, to say the least. The lowest grade she had ever received on anything was a B-minus, and she cried for an entire hour after finding out.

Determined to make this turn out all right, she decided to talk to Mr. Chu after class. Surely, he would not punish *her* with the bad grade. She had been the only one to do any real work.

The bell rang, and Dee approached Mr. Chu. "Does everyone in the group get the same grade?" she asked.

"Yes, that is correct," came his reply.

"So, I also get a D?" Dee's voice was quavering, and she tried not to cry.

"I'm afraid so. The lesson was less about the research and more about working together, as I mentioned during class. Your group did not work together very well at all; your ability to cooperate was well below average. Don't worry, though. This is a skill we will work on in class."

"But, I worked hard on my part," Dee pleaded.

"Yes, that was obvious, so I am sure this is disappointing for you. Working together is an important skill that is necessary for future success. When you are older, you will need to get along, and work, with different types of people. Group work at school helps to build those necessary skills. That was the lesson."

Dee was too angry to cry. *I'm not a grown-up! I won't be out working with anyone for a long time. This is so dumb!* Her thoughts were racing.

Mr. Chu wrote her a pass to get to her next class. She took it and hurried out.

She was exhausted by the time she got home that afternoon. It was the weekend, so that was something to be grateful for. Sue called, and they made plans for the next day.

"Should we invite Ronnie and Samantha?" Sue asked with a happy tone.

"NO!" Dee shouted. "Samantha, yes, but no Ronnie!"

"Okay, okay! But you'd better tell me why when I see you tomorrow."

"I will. See you then." Dee didn't think she could keep the story inside her even if she tried. Her feelings were like a volcano, ready to erupt!

CHAPTER SEVEN

GOODBYE, FANTASTIC FOUR

Dee and Samantha met over at Sue's the next day. Samantha was especially happy. Math class was going well, as a result of the tutoring sessions with Penny.

"Penny's amazing!" Samantha said. "Dee, your mom helped me last year, and this year I have Penny. The two best tutors in the whole world!"

Dee managed a small smile; she was happy to hear that Samantha was having a better start to the year. Fifth grade had been difficult for her. If anyone deserved a turn of luck, it was Samantha.

"I'm glad," Dee said. "I wish Penny could help me with my problems. Although, I have so many, I wouldn't know where to start!"

"Yeah, Dee. What's going on with you and Ronnie?" Sue asked. "You sounded so mad at her last night."

Dee told the others the entire story. "She made our group get a D on our project! She's so conceited, too. Oh, and she flips her hair like this now." Dee demonstrated the movement; although, with her fine blonde hair, it didn't have quite the same effect. "And that's not all. She hardly talks to me, and when she does, it's like she doesn't like me at all!"

Sue and Samantha looked surprised at this outburst of Dee's. "Did you do something to make Ronnie mad?" Samantha asked.

"No—at least I don't think so. She's different now. SO different!"

Neither Samantha nor Sue had heard from Ronnie, either. As a group, they wondered if this meant that the Fantastic Four was a thing of the past.

"I don't care if Ronnie is part of the group anymore. I don't think anyone who's mean should be in it," Dee declared.

"I'd like to wait and see if Ronnie gets over it," Sue said thoughtfully. "I can't understand why she's acting so strange. It doesn't make sense."

"I could call her," Samantha offered.

"She isn't answering my calls, but maybe she'll answer yours," Sue said.

And so, it was decided. Samantha would call Ronnie and get back to the others if she found out anything.

"How's Andrew been?" Sue asked Dee.

"Andrew is such a nuisance," Dee said. "He screwed up our project grade, too, by talking about beer!"

"Beer?" Samantha was shocked.

"Beer," Dee confirmed. "And, you should've seen the fight he was in during the first week of school." The girls went on to discuss the fight that had occurred between Nolan and Andrew.

"Maybe Andrew will stop bullying others," Samantha said. "He's been a jerk, especially to you, Dee."

"Actually, Andrew didn't start the fight. I was there. Nolan pushed Andrew into me! That's what started the whole thing. Andrew got a cut on his arm, too. I didn't like seeing him get beat up by Nolan, even if he is a jerk." Dee stopped. "Wait! Why am I feeling sorry for him?"

"Beats me!" Sue said with a chuckle. "Hey, let's get some ice cream!"

The ice cream party lightened everyone's mood. Dee was feeling better about everything. It helped to talk with her friends.

Later that evening, Samantha called to report back to Dee about what had happened with Ronnie. Samantha had called Ronnie twice. The first time she left a message on the answering machine, and the second time she spoke to Mrs. McCormick and left a message with her. Ronnie's mother seemed as pleasant as always, so Samantha thought that, maybe, there was hope that nothing serious was wrong.

Dee decided that instead of sulking, she would try to find out more on her own. She didn't know how, but she would get to the bottom of it!

* * *

Dee kept an eye on Ronnie for the next couple of weeks and wrote down her observations on a piece of paper:

1. Ronnie hasn't called any of us.

2. She hangs around with Brenda and another girl a lot.

3. *She constantly does the hair-flipping thing.*

4. *She still avoids me.*

So far, there wasn't anything new happening with Ronnie—good *or* bad. She just didn't seem interested in being friends with her old group.

As time went on, everyone settled into cliques. Ronnie's clique seemed to be the popular group. Dee's group was what was left of the Fantastic Four. Andrew was in the "annoying-boy" group.

One day, Dee spotted something in a corner of the cafeteria during lunch. A group of tall boys was talking and laughing with someone. Dee walked a little closer to get a better look. *No!* Right in the center of the group was none other than Ronnie!

She always did talk a lot about boys, but Dee had thought it was because Ronnie had an older brother. *Oh, wow. There goes the flirty hair-flip.* Dee was stunned and froze in place. Ronnie looked over and saw Dee but didn't wave.

Dee decided to find out more about those boys. She didn't know any of them, but Sue might.

The bell then rang, and the students left the cafeteria.

That night, Dee called Sue and relayed the information. Sue seemed surprised that Ronnie would be so friendly with boys. Sue and Dee had found them to be annoying. The friends teased each other about boys from time to time, but neither was all that interested in them yet. Dee promised to point out those particular boys at lunch if she saw them again.

The next day, Dee was able to point out the boys to

Sue. They were easy to spot now. All she had to do was look for the redheaded girl in their midst.

"I know two of them!" Sue exclaimed. "They're EIGHTH-GRADERS! Their gym class was combined with my class when their teacher was out sick. We had to try to throw the ball to someone standing on a platform while others tried to get the ball first...."

"Eighth-graders?" Dee interrupted, not quite believing what she had heard.

"Yeah, and they were good at the game. I think they're pretty popular. All the girls were gaga over them." Sue sighed. "How did Ronnie get into *that* group?"

Dee felt a little jealous. The only attention she had gotten from any boy was teasing from Andrew. Ronnie's making it into the popular group was the icing on the cake. It wasn't bad enough that Ronnie was ignoring her and had been largely responsible for her getting the worst grade of her life. Now Ronnie had suddenly become too "good" to be friends with Dee, Sue, or Samantha.

"I think we should just give up. Ronnie doesn't like us anymore." Dee looked very sad.

"We were once the Terrific Trio. We could be that again," Sue offered, trying to cheer Dee up.

"No, that name won't work because Ronnie was part of that group. We need a new name." They both were quiet for quite a while, trying to think of one.

"How about the Thoughtful Three?" Sue suggested.

"Too serious. How about the Thrilling Three? Or the Thorny Three? I certainly feel thorny lately," Dee said with a chuckle.

Sue shook her head. "Well, the Thrilling Three sounds

okay. Let's ask Samantha what she thinks. Where is she, anyway?"

"I haven't seen her. I'll call her tonight."

* * *

Dee told Samantha all that she had discovered about Ronnie when they chatted that night.

"Whoa," Samantha said. "Ronnie was always boy-crazy, but I didn't think she was like *this*: hanging around with boys and flirting with them."

"Well, I don't care if she never comes back to our group! She doesn't like us anyway. Sue and I were trying to think of a new name for our group. We can't be the Fantastic Four anymore because now there are only three of us. I thought of the Thrilling Three. What do you think?" Dee asked.

The line went silent. "Are you still there?"

"Yup," Samantha replied. "I have a dictionary, and I'm looking up words that start with 'T'. Ooh! How about Trendy Trio?"

"What does 'trendy' mean?"

"The dictionary says it means 'very fashionable'," Samantha said, "and 'fashionable' means—wait a second—'stylish'."

"Fashionable? Stylish? Us? It's kind of weird, but I like it! Let's ask Sue if she thinks we're more thrilling or trendy."

"She'll likely think we lost our minds!"

"Excellent!" Dee exclaimed. "I hope she picks your idea. 'Trendy' is way cooler!"

Samantha offered to call Sue. When all was said and

done, the new group Trendy Trio was born!

Dee finally reached a degree of acceptance about Ronnie. Friendship is a two-way street. If one person wants to break away from the group, the friendship is over with that person. Having chatted with Sue and Samantha, Dee felt certain that the other two-thirds of the Trendy Trio were very good friends. That was one problem off her list. It was time to tackle the next one... her History grade.

CHAPTER EIGHT

PROBLEM LIST

Dee had never received a grade of D before, so she didn't know what would be required to bring such a grade up to an A. She wanted to ask Mr. Chu what she needed to do, but she was still upset about how he had handled the grading of the project. Punishing the one who worked the hardest the same as the ones who did nothing *or* the wrong thing didn't seem right. She would figure out a way to fix this.

One afternoon when Dee was at Samantha's house, Penny came over to drop off some worksheets for Samantha. Penny then joined the girls for a couple of minutes. "Dee, how do you like middle school?" she inquired.

Dee took a huge breath. "It's going okay after a rough start. One of our friends left our group. I'm over it now, but she messed up a History project our group was doing, and we all got a bad grade." Dee had a sudden brainstorm. She would ask Penny how to go from a D to an A in a class! After all, Penny was older and, Dee hoped, wiser. "The project grade was a D. How can I bring my average up to an A?"

Penny was thoughtfully silent for a short time. "Make History your priority this term. Do all your homework really well. Participate in class discussions. Teachers really like students who share opinions and ask interesting questions. Study for all your tests. You'll have that grade up to an A in no time!"

Dee was grateful for the advice, but she wasn't sure about class participation. She was shy, and talking in front of others in *this* class made her nervous. However, she trusted Penny's opinion, so she would try.

In History class, they had been talking about the two sets of fathers and sons who had been President. The first pair was President John Adams, the father, and President John Quincy Adams, the son. Mr. Chu focused on them during class time. The homework was to research the second pair: President George Bush, the father, and President George W. Bush, the son. Dee had spent a long time doing her homework so that she could answer some questions in class the next day.

The discussion began. Some of the more confident students answered Mr. Chu's questions before Dee could muster up the courage to say anything. There were only a few minutes left in class. She hoped the next question would be easy.

"Which President do you think was the better one?" Mr. Chu asked.

Dee decided to go for it. She raised her hand and was acknowledged. "I'm not sure which one was better because both Presidents had problems to try to fix, but I think George W. Bush had the worst problem because of 9/11. His father didn't have a terrorism problem to solve, but there was a war then."

Mr. Chu seemed delighted with Dee's thoughtful answer and told her so. He went on to talk about the stresses of being a country's leader when war or terrorism occurs. The bell interrupted him, and class was over before homework could be assigned.

Dee was happy for the night off from History homework. Others in the class were as well.

"Nice going, Dee," Andrew said. "If you didn't answer that question, Mr. Chu might have remembered to give us homework." He put his hand up for a high-five as they left the room. Dee went to reciprocate the high-five, but Andrew pulled his hand away playfully before it met hers. He flashed her a mischievous smile.

Whatever! Just when I think he's being nice!

Dee suddenly felt confident that she could bring up her History grade. She always completed homework assignments and passed them in on time. Every test was studied for. Now she had broken the barrier of fear and would keep offering opinions during class discussions. It was a little challenging for her because Ronnie and Andrew were in the class. However, her desire for good grades was the priority. If they didn't like what she said, it didn't matter to her anymore.

Thinking of her list of problems, she had determined that Ronnie was no longer interested in a friendship and had decided to let it go. She now had a plan to improve her History grade, so she felt better about that. One problem that could not be fixed was missing Pete. He had gone to a different school, and Dee knew she had no control over that. She thought of calling Pete to say hi, but then Andrew would find out.

Andrew. Of course! He was the next problem Dee would try to tackle. It might just be her biggest challenge yet!

* * *

Andrew Burke was problem number three on Dee's list. Her mother had once said, "We can control only our own thoughts and actions. We do not have any control over what anyone else does." If that was true, then was there any hope of fixing this problem?

What was it about Andrew that bothered her so much? She decided to make a list.

<u>Problems with Andrew</u>

1. He's annoying

2. He made fun of me all last year

3. He messed up our project grade

4. He's a jerk in class

5. He teases me about Pete

Dee looked the list over. He certainly was a pest, but it wasn't clear how anything she could do or say would change any of the things on the list. *Mom might be right.* She decided to ask her parents about it. She put the list in her jeans pocket.

After dinner that night, Dee asked her parents if she could get their help with something. They agreed. Joey was encouraged to find something else to do, and he left the kitchen. The other three remained seated around the table.

"What is it, Dee?" Mrs. Lanson asked with concern.

Dee proceeded to tell them the whole story. She took the now crinkled-up piece of paper from her pocket and showed it to her mom, who then passed it to her dad.

"Hmm," Mr. Lanson said, but that was all.

"This is quite a list," Mrs. Lanson commented. "What do you want the outcome to be?"

Dee thought that should be obvious. "What do you mean?" she asked, a bit confused.

"Well, do you want this boy to just leave you alone, or do you want him to be nicer to you? As I said, you need to decide what you want the outcome to be."

"Well, I don't know. I want him to stop being a pest. Dad, what do you think?" Dee asked, hoping for some help from him.

"Boys are immature in middle school, but you might not need to worry about him much longer." He looked sad as he said it, leaving Dee feeling more confused—and now upset about what he had meant by it.

"Thanks. I guess I'll think about this some more." Dee got up from the table and went to her room.

What was that all about? I 'might not need to worry about him much longer.' Dad is sure acting weird! She felt tired. Suddenly, she had an idea. *Penny! She will help me if I ask her!*

Dee called Samantha and asked her to set up a time so that she could talk with Penny. "You can be there, too, because you know how Andrew is." Samantha promised to try to arrange it.

She called right back. "Penny's coming over tomorrow

for my math lesson. Meet us here at 4:00. She said she'd be happy to help."

"Thanks. I'll check with Mom, but I'm sure it'll be okay."

The next day, Dee put the list in her pocket and went over to Samantha's house. Penny greeted Dee with a warm smile. Dee felt at ease immediately and began to describe her dilemma.

"That's quite a story," Penny said. She took a deep breath.

"And, Dee isn't exaggerating at all! I heard a lot of his teasing when we played softball last year. And this year, he came to our table at lunch and started bugging Dee. Teasing her about Pete—one of his friends—and then he started making kissing noises. Yuck!"

Penny laughed. "I think I might know what the problem is. My guess is that Andrew has a crush on you, Dee."

Dee's eyes widened in disbelief. "NO WAY!"

"Just when you thought the Andrew problem couldn't get any worse!" Samantha tried not to laugh, but she couldn't help it.

"I hope he doesn't like me, because I don't like him!" She turned to Penny. "What makes you think he likes me? He acts just the opposite."

"Experience," Penny said with a smile. "Do you like him at all?"

"No. Not one bit!"

"Okay. You could try ignoring him. If I'm wrong, and he's annoying you for no good reason, then he might stop. If I'm right and he likes you, he will act upset that you're not giving him any attention. He might even try to be nice."

"He's hard to ignore because we're in three classes

together. *Three!"* Dee emphasized.

"If he stopped talking to you, would you be okay with that?" Penny asked.

"Yes! I would be the happiest sixth-grader in the world!"

* * *

Penny had given Dee something to think about. *Andrew likes me? That would be a huge nightmare!* This new theory kept her awake that night. She was trying to figure out what to do.

She got up early the next morning and wrote a new list.

<u>Andrew</u>

1. Bugs me worst at lunch

2. Bugs me sometimes after class

3. Bugs me least in math

4. Bugs me mostly about Pete

5. I wish he would GO AWAY!

Dee didn't see any hint of Andrew's liking her hiding anywhere in this list. It was unthinkable. *Number 4 – He teases me mostly about Pete. If Andrew likes me, why would he tease me about somebody else? No, it's impossible.* She stuffed the list into her backpack and left for the bus.

The first class of the day was English. Andrew was in that class, but he sat on the other side of the room. Sue was in the class, too. Dee made a mental note to ask her if she had noticed anything.

Dee took out the English binder from her backpack to get ready for class. She had to dig deep to find a pencil. Turning to Sue, she mouthed the words, "I want to talk to you after class." Sue nodded.

The class went by at a snail's pace. They were learning, once again, about nouns, which she had done every year since she was six years old. *Boring!* Finally, the bell rang, and she packed up her bag and met Sue.

"I have to ask you something," she whispered.

Suddenly, Andrew came charging up behind her. "Dee, you dropped this!" he exclaimed. Just as she turned to see what he wanted, she saw him unfolding a paper and reading it.

"Here! Take it!" he yelled, as he pushed through the crowd and all but ran away.

Dee knew immediately what paper it was—the "Andrew" list. After reading it, he had looked hurt and mad. *Uh-oh! Now what do I do?*

"What do you want to talk to me about?" Sue asked.

"I think I just got the answer to the question I was going to ask you. I'll call you later."

Dee saw Andrew several more times that day. He hardly talked to anyone and ignored Dee totally. She hadn't seen this coming. Maybe he did like her after all, as Penny had said. Then, Dee remembered her father's comment about middle-school boys being immature. Maybe he was just immature and doing stupid "boy" pranks. Maybe he didn't like her after all, but now she had hurt his feelings and embarrassed herself. That just might be worse than his teasing.

She called Sue later that day and told her the whole story.

"Yikes!" Sue exclaimed. "This is crazy! I don't even know what to say! Do you think he LIKES you? Ew!"

"I'm not sure. But if he did, he doesn't like me anymore!"

"Let's see if he tries to talk to you again," Sue suggested.

"I guess," Dee said. "I just feel bad and dumb at the same time."

"Anyway, he'll get over it eventually," Sue said. She announced that her mom was calling her to supper, so the conversation ended.

The next couple of weeks were uncomfortable for Dee as she waited for trouble from Andrew. That never happened. He didn't talk to her at all, but he also didn't seem to hold a grudge. Dee wondered if she should apologize, but she couldn't seem to get up the courage. Once in History class, he had ended up in her group for a mini-project. He didn't tease her or say anything about the list. He kept the conversation to the project and was not unpleasant at all.

At home, Dee took inventory of her earlier problem list. The Ronnie and History grade problems had resolved. Now, it seemed that the Andrew problem had worked itself out also. She wouldn't have chosen to embarrass herself in that way—with Andrew finding the list—but the teasing had stopped. That was all she wanted. Andrew had seemed to get over it. So, it was all good. Right? She hoped so.

Suddenly, she felt better about everything. She could finally relax and enjoy life as a middle-schooler!

CHAPTER NINE

NO WAY!

Dee and Joey were playing a rare game of Monopoly. It was a rainy Saturday, and Dee had managed to convince Joey to play against her. He hadn't quite mastered the winning technique, and so he always lost. Unbeknownst to Dee, he had looked up some strategies online and was confident in his newfound knowledge. He would beat her today!

Mrs. Lanson entered the room and took a deep breath. "Your dad and I would like to talk with you about something. Please come into the dining room." Her tone was serious.

Dee and Joey looked at each other. Were they in trouble? Family meetings were never about fun things.

The one that came to Dee's mind was the grand announcement that an addition would be put on the house. That summer was full of banging and drilling—so much noise—as walls were torn down and new ones constructed. The end result was fine, but it had been inconvenient—Dee even got sent to camp while her bedroom was being worked on.

"Mom," Joey whined. "We're playing a game. Can we do the meeting later?"

"Yeah, Mom," Dee pleaded.

Mrs. Lanson shook her head. "Please come now."

They gathered around the dining room table. No one spoke at first, and the silence just added to the suspense.

"Dee and Joey," Mr. Lanson began, "you are the best kids in the world! Your mother and I love you so much."

"You brought us in here to tell us that?" Joey laughed. "You don't need a meeting for that; you say it a lot!"

"It's because we love you that we want you included in every step of our plan," Mrs. Lanson added.

Plan? Dee didn't like the sound of this. "What plan?" she inquired suspiciously.

"The bosses at work have decided to move our entire company to Florida," Mr. Lanson said, trying to sound upbeat.

"That's too bad. So where will you work, then?" Dee asked.

"Well..." Mr. Lanson paused. "I will be working for the same company, and we will be moving to Florida!" he stated cautiously but enthusiastically.

Dee's mouth dropped open, and Joey stared down at the table.

"I'm not moving!" Joey protested.

"Neither am I," Dee said. "We are *not* moving!" Tears welled up in her eyes.

Mrs. Lanson spoke in a gentle tone. "It won't happen

immediately. In fact, we have a family vacation planned, to go to Florida and see what it would be like to live there. It's warm and beautiful, with nice beaches and pretty palm trees. Once we see it for ourselves, the transition will be easier."

"NO!" screamed Joey. "I don't want to go. I won't go!" He stormed out of the room with Dee right behind him.

Mr. and Mrs. Lanson decided not to go after them. The children needed time to adjust to the news.

Dee and Joey returned to their game but didn't play. Dee was crying now, and Joey aggressively pushed the Monopoly board away, sending all the properties, money, and game pieces flying across the room.

"How could they do this to us?" Dee sobbed.

Joey shook his head. "I'm not going. They can't make me!"

"They *can* make us; that's the problem. We're just kids. We have no say."

"We'll see about that," Joey said. He stormed off to his room.

Dee retreated to her room as well. She lay on her bed and stared at the ceiling. She didn't know what to think— her mind had so many thoughts going through it. She had finally reached the point of feeling happy at school. All the problems she had faced seemed minor compared to this.

If we move, I'll lose my friends. The Trendy Trio will be ruined, and only Samantha and Sue will be left in the group. I'll have no friends and will have to go to a new school where I won't know anyone. This is the worst thing that could happen to me! Dee cried, wondering how her parents could do this to her. The tears kept coming as she felt sadder and sadder.

Suddenly, she had an idea. *That's it—I need to talk to Penny! She'll know what to do.* Dee's mood lightened.

Joey, on the other hand, experienced no improvement in mood. He didn't speak to anyone at supper that night and returned to his room immediately afterward.

It was Joey's night to help with the dishes, but Dee stepped in for him. "Mom, I'll dry the dishes tonight. Joey can do it for me tomorrow."

Maybe if I'm really good, they'll change their minds. It was worth a try.

* * *

The next morning, Mrs. Lanson knocked on Dee's and Joey's bedroom doors—reminding them to get up and ready for church.

Dee came to the breakfast table and quietly ate her breakfast. Joey was a no-show.

"Where's Joey?" Mr. Lanson asked when he came into the kitchen.

Dee shrugged her shoulders. "Am I my brother's keeper?" She was proud of herself for remembering a passage from the Bible.

Mr. Lanson ruffled her hair and left the kitchen in search of Joey. "Eileen, have you seen Joey? He doesn't seem to be in the house anywhere." There was a hint of concern in his voice.

A further search revealed that Joey was gone—vanished.

"Joe, what are we going to do? He's not here." Mrs. Lanson felt panicked. "He was so upset about the move."

"Let's not jump to conclusions," Mr. Lanson cautioned.

"Dee, did Joey say anything to you?"

"Nope," Dee said, "but I'll help you look. Maybe he's hiding out back."

They all went outside and looked around but found no trace of Joey. Mrs. Lanson returned to the house and began calling neighbors and Joey's friends who lived in the vicinity, but no one had seen him.

Joey had a habit of wandering off during outings when something grabbed his attention, but this felt different. Very different. He had been so angry and upset. His absence could be an act of defiance....

Mrs. Lanson ran to find her husband. "I think I know where he is," she declared. "The woods off Cosmer Street."

While Mrs. Lanson made more calls, Mr. Lanson offered to check it out. He headed toward the forbidden area. First, he searched along the paths and was relieved in a way when he didn't find him. These woods were a dangerous place for children wandering around alone. He thought about turning back and going home, but his instinct made him search on.

Leaves rustling a distance away caught his attention, and he moved in the direction of the noise. He rounded the bend and nearly collided with Dee! "What are you doing in here?" he shouted.

"I thought Joey might have come here, and I found him. I was going back home to tell you. He looked cold but said that he's not going back. Come on—I'll show you."

Mr. Lanson decided not to reprimand Dee just yet about coming to the woods. She had found Joey, after all.

They approached Joey, who was sitting against a rock and shivering from the cold.

"Son," Mr. Lanson said gently, "what are you doing out

here?" Noticing Joey's shivers, Mr. Lanson removed his jacket and placed it around his son's shoulders. It made Joey look so small, wrapped up in the man-size jacket.

Joey moved away from his father and looked in the opposite direction.

"I'm sorry if you're upset about moving to Florida. Relocating the business was not my idea."

Joey looked up with sad eyes. "So, you don't want to move either?"

"Well, we just put the addition on our house, so I guess I wasn't thinking of moving."

"So, we can stay? Please say we can stay," Joey pleaded.

"Yeah, Dad! Please, can we stay?" Dee echoed.

"Let's take this Florida vacation and see how we like the area. Your mother and I want you and Dee in on every-thing." He hugged Joey close.

Dee smiled at this. She liked to feel included in things. Her vote would remain "no," as she was sure Joey's vote would also.

"Can we do some fun stuff in Florida?" Joey asked.

"You bet!" Mr. Lanson said. "Let's go home, kids."

As a result of all the excitement, they missed going to church.

Dee sat in the living room alone, trying to process this new information. She was stunned by it, to say the least. She guessed that the company's plan to move to Florida might have been what had made her father act so strangely. She couldn't help but be angry about the whole thing. The changes she would have to endure were not making her happy. *A new house. A new school. No friends. What about Sue and Samantha? And Penny?*

Tears welled up in her eyes. How would she ever be

able to tell her friends that she might be moving so far away? The thought of it was totally upsetting. She hoped her parents would change their minds so that she wouldn't have to say anything.

CHAPTER TEN

NOT A FASHION SHOW

Dee returned to school the next day with a heavy heart. She couldn't imagine living in Florida. The weather there was almost always hot and humid—the exact conditions she hated. However, the idea of starting over in a new school with no friends was troubling her the most. She could maybe tolerate the heat if she had Sue and Samantha to hang around with.

"Hey, what's up?" Sue had come up from behind, and Dee had failed to notice.

"Nothing," Dee sighed.

"It sure looks like something. Is everything all right?"

"Yeah. I just have to get to class." Dee hurried away.

"Hey, wait up!" Sue ran to catch up with her. "What's wrong? We tell each other everything. Tell me! What's going on?"

For once, Dee didn't feel like saying one word about a problem. She usually shared with her friends everything that was on her mind, but this was different. The thought of moving was so painful; she found herself mute on the subject.

"Don't worry," she told Sue. "I'm good."

"Okay. I've got to get to class. See ya!" Sue sprinted away.

The school year now had a flow and sense of order to it. Classes were combinations of lectures, discussions, hands-on activities, tests, and homework. If a student completed all tasks, then grades were generally good.

Dee found it easier to manage school now that Ronnie and Andrew weren't stressing her out. In spite of this, though, the move hovered over her like a dark cloud; part of her wished it would just rain and get it over with. The scouting-out vacation was still a couple of weeks away. Skipping ahead to living in Florida might be easier than the torture of seeing all that she would be leaving behind.

"Delores, could I see you for a moment after class?" Ms. Hersh whispered as Dee walked into the room.

"Sure," Dee replied and sat down. Wondering what Ms. Hersh wanted made her curious. *Moving to Florida means no more Ms. Hersh! One good thing.* Dee amused herself with the thought that if she listed the benefits of moving, that would be the only item on the list.

After class, Dee approached the teacher's desk and waited for the next problem that was about to be unearthed.

"Delores, your grades have been slipping over the last couple of weeks. I'm concerned. Are you having difficulty with the material?"

"No, I don't think so," Dee uttered.

Ms. Hersh handed Dee her last test—70 percent. Dee understood that a 70 is a C-minus and just one point away from a D. "Is everything all right, Delores?"

No, everything is NOT all right! "I'm okay. I'll try to do better." Suddenly, Dee had a brilliant idea. "My friend has a tutor. Maybe I could work with her."

"Excellent! I will make that recommendation right away. Hopefully, you can get started before the holiday break. Now, here is a pass to your next class."

Dee imagined working with Penny and felt instantly better.

Upon arriving home, she noticed her mother looking perplexed. Perhaps her mother was feeling upset about the move, too. "Dee, please come and sit down."

Dee obeyed, hoping her mom would reveal that the move was off.

"I was contacted by Ms. Hersh today about securing you a tutor. She was emphatic that the lessons should begin today. You've never had trouble in math. What's this about?"

"Oh, I got a couple low grades, and she thought I needed help before Christmas break."

Mrs. Lanson looked skeptical. "Well, the tutor is due here any minute. Grab a snack and get ready."

For the first time since the bad news was revealed, Dee felt glad. She was eager to see Penny.

The doorbell rang. Mrs. Lanson went to answer the door while Dee set up for the lesson.

"Hi, Pen..." Dee stopped in mid-sentence.

"Hi Dee, I'm Caitlyn. I hear you need help with math."

"I'm sorry, but I'm supposed to work with Penny."

"No, your math teacher asked me to do it. Let's talk about what you don't understand, and then we can get started."

"No!" Dee barked. "I don't need help. I'm smart and know the math. I need to talk to *Penny*!"

Caitlyn was flabbergasted. "Your teacher told me you needed help. I don't understand."

"Well, I *don't* need help!" Dee put her head down and refused to say another word.

Mrs. Lanson heard the commotion and came to settle the dispute. She heard both sides, and then dismissed Caitlyn after paying her for the unfulfilled session.

"What's going on?" Mrs. Lanson demanded. "It is not like you to be so rude."

Dee pouted and ignored her mother for a couple of minutes. "I don't want to move!" she declared finally. "It's all I think about. I got a bad test grade—whoopee do—so Ms. Hersh got all bent out of shape. She said I need a tutor, and I said yes because I thought it would be Penny. I didn't need her help; I needed a friend. Other than Sue and Samantha."

"I see," Mrs. Lanson began.

"No, you don't see. Because if you did, you wouldn't make us move!"

"I'm truly sorry that this has upset you so much. It may surprise you that I feel sad as well."

"Really?" Dee wiped her eyes.

"I have friends and a community that I will be missing, too. This is very hard on all of us, but we must stick together and help one another," Mrs. Lanson encouraged.

"How am I going to tell Sue and Samantha? I don't think I can do it!" Dee gasped to catch her breath.

"Their mothers are my friends. I could be the one to break the news."

"Would you?" Dee pleaded. "I just can't."

"Yes, Dee. I will, but it won't be easy for me, either. I just might lose it myself!" Mrs. Lanson hugged her daughter.

Dee lay awake that night, wondering what would happen when the news broke. She hoped it wouldn't be as hard to face Sue and Samantha as she imagined. Would it be sad? Awkward? Terrible? It was only a matter of time before the answer would be revealed, and the thought of it terrified her.

* * *

The next day, Samantha bounded up to Dee. "Can you come over later? Mom said she would take us out shopping. Maybe we can be weird and all buy the same shirt! We are the Trendy Trio, after all!"

Dee was surprised that Samantha was so happy. Perhaps she had not yet heard the news. "Sure! That sounds like fun. I'll check with Mom, but she'll probably say yes."

There was a bounce in Dee's step as she went through the day. She was so excited for the chance to spend time with her friends. Imagining buying the same shirt was weird enough to bring a smile to her face. Even her classes seemed more interesting, and she vowed to work harder until the break.

After school, Mrs. Perry took Samantha, Sue, and Dee to the mall. They wandered around the various shops and tried on some clothes. "Hey, let's look for the wackiest outfit we can find and model it for each other!" Sue had a silly streak, apparently.

Dee and Samantha squealed in delight. The challenge

was on! Each girl tried to conceal from the others the clothes she had found.

"Okay," Sue declared. "Put your clothes in a dressing room. Mrs. Perry, can you guard the dressing rooms with our stuff in them while we take turns modeling?"

Mrs. Perry nodded, and Sue turned to the others. "I'll go first."

Samantha and Dee giggled while they waited for Sue to emerge in wacky outfit number one. It seemed like forever, but the fitting room door finally did open. Sue came out, walking like a model, wearing a hideous outfit.

Laughter abounded as they all took in the sight before them. Sue was wearing a long green skirt, hot pink T-shirt, wide-brimmed brown hat, yellow sweater, and bright pink sneakers!

"My eyes are going crazy with all those colors," Dee guffawed. "I think I need sunglasses!"

"I'd say blinders! Sue, that's bad!" Samantha covered her eyes. "I'll go next."

Dee stood alone with Mrs. Perry while Sue changed back into her normal clothes and Samantha changed into her chosen outfit. Mrs. Perry didn't let on that she knew anything about the move. Dee felt happy and was having fun with her friends.

"Watch out, world!" Samantha came bounding out of the fitting room and spun around dramatically. She had on baggy purple pants with an oversized yellow sweatshirt and a white bandana. The high-heeled shoes got caught on the bottom of the baggy pants, and she nearly tipped over.

Dee laughed so hard that she could barely speak. She grabbed the hat from Sue and put it on Samantha. "There!

Now you look like you belong out in a field, scaring away crows!"

"Except for the heels!" Sue chuckled. "You're up next, Dee!"

Dee's outfit was a complete surprise. She had skillfully covered up the clothes with a plain navy-blue skirt. "Are you ready for wacky outfit number three?" she called.

"Ready!" the other girls chorused.

Dee emerged and sauntered by them, slowly turning so that they could take it all in.

"OMG!" shouted Samantha.

"Whoa!" squealed Sue.

"What's the matter—don't you like plaid?" Dee quipped.

She had on bright orange plaid pants and a neon pink plaid blouse, with a blue flannel, button-down plaid shirt over that. Around her neck was a tan plaid winter scarf, and she was wearing gray plaid mittens.

"Take it off!" screeched Samantha.

"Dee, you win the prize for THE wackiest outfit!" Sue shook her head. "I can't believe that so many ugly things could be found in one store!"

Mrs. Perry suggested that they go for an ice cream next, but Samantha vetoed the idea. "Mom, we have to get our T-shirts first."

The girls went to a shop that specialized in custom T-shirts. Pictures, words, or phrases could be printed on the shirts.

"Let's get the same color and have the same saying on it," suggested Samantha. It had been her idea, after all, so the other girls agreed. After studying the wide range of colors, they chose medium blue.

"What should we write on it?" Dee asked.

Sue gazed at her with wide eyes. "'Trendy Trio', of course!"

"Great!" exclaimed Samantha. "What color letters?"

"How about gold or silver?" Dee wanted the shirt to look fancy and special. The worker who was assisting them suggested silver as the better match.

Sue, Dee, and Samantha watched as one and then another shirt came out from under the heated press. They giggled with anticipation. Finally, the shirts were ready, and the girls paid for them.

"Can we wear them now?" Samantha asked her mother.

"Where will you change?" Mrs. Perry inquired.

The worker pointed to a fitting room, and the girls ran for it, their shirts in their hands. They took turns, and before they knew it, the Trendy Trio girls were ready to go for their ice creams.

There was one booth left, and the girls rushed over and sat down. It had been an enjoyable outing for them. Each had a turn telling her favorite part.

Eventually, Mrs. Perry looked at her watch and declared that it was time to leave. As they stepped out into the mall, they almost collided with a group of boys.

"Dee?" one voice called out.

Dee looked at the speaker and nearly fainted. "Pete! What are you doing here?"

"We're going for ice cream!" he said. "What's new?"

"Not much," Dee fibbed.

The other boys tapped their feet impatiently.

"Gotta go. Nice to see you all! By the way, nice shirts!"

Seeing Pete made Dee's day even better. He was still nice to her, even though she bet Andrew had told him all about the incident with the list. She no longer cared a jot about Andrew. She wished that she could have asked Pete about his new school. Maybe she would see him again. She hoped so!

CHAPTER ELEVEN

PROBLEM LIST REVENGE

Dee returned to school with a renewed burst of energy. Confident in her math abilities, she would work hard to bring up her average, which had been brought down by the two low test grades. She didn't need the help of a tutor. She knew how to study math. The answer was quite simple: study the notes and do practice problems.

During lunch, the Trendy Trio again discussed their fun outing at the mall. Every time they spoke of the wild outfits they had modeled, they would break into take-your-breath-away laughter.

"Wasn't it weird to see Pete?" Samantha asked, just as Andrew walked by them with his lunch tray.

Dee waited for him to pass. "Yeah. I was surprised, all right! I wonder if he likes his new school."

"You could always ask Andrew," Sue teased.

"Ask me what?" Andrew said, on his way to get napkins to clean up a minor spill.

"Nothing." Dee stared at the table, hoping he would just go away. He shrugged his shoulders and left.

"That was close!" Samantha whispered.

Dee looked at her friends and wondered just how they would feel when they heard about the move.

As if reading her mind, Sue began, "Don't look so sad. We already know. Our moms told us."

"You know?... About the move?" Dee stuttered.

"Yes. It's really sad for us, too." Samantha paused in an attempt to keep from crying. "That's why we went out shopping—to cheer us all up."

"It worked. I had a lot of fun," Dee said.

Sue bopped her hand against Dee's hand. "You'll have to invite us to visit. Maybe we could spend the summer with you."

That was a mood-lifter if ever there was one. "Of course, you can come! And what if we send snail mail instead of email? Would the Trendy Trio be so weird as to do something so old-fashioned?" Dee laughed.

"Let's do it!" Sue agreed. "That would be weird, but fun too! My mom told me that when she was our age, she used to have pen pals who would write to her. She said it was fun to get letters in the mail."

"I'm in! Then, maybe someday our parents will buy us all smartphones, and we can video chat," Samantha added.

"Well, we'll have a long wait. My parents told me that I can't get a smartphone until I'm in high school." Dee rolled her eyes and shook her head in frustration.

"Hey, no downers! High school will be here before we know it," Sue encouraged her.

Just then, the bell rang, and the group scattered to their next classes.

At home, Dee worked hard on her homework and

studied for every test. Her grades in math improved dramatically, in just a short time.

She sat looking out the window as she wondered how the family vacation would be. She hoped that no one would like Florida, and her parents would call off the move and make life right once again.

* * *

The last day of school before the holiday break had arrived. Students were noisier than ever; the crowds in the halls seemed to be worse. Dee couldn't wait for the day to end.

Math was the last class of the day, and Ms. Hersh allowed them to work on a math puzzle to "celebrate" the upcoming vacation. It was tricky, and by the end of class, Dee was the only one who had figured it out.

The dismissal bell rang, and the students clamored to beat one another out the door. Ms. Hersh took Dee aside and quietly congratulated her for bringing her math average up to a B-plus. Dee hoped that she could improve it to an A by the second week in January, when the term would be over.

As she walked out into the hall, she noticed Andrew just standing there. "You dropped this." He handed her a piece of paper.

"Thanks," she said, but she didn't remember dropping anything. She opened up the folded paper.

THINGS THAT BUG ME
ABOUT DEE

EVERYTHING

When she looked up, he was gone.

How annoying! Oh, he had been nice to me, while scheming and planning this dirty trick. Dee crinkled up the note and shoved it into her bag. *Wait until Sue and Samantha see this!*

At home, she was so angry that she couldn't even eat the cookies her mother had baked for her and Joey, to celebrate their last day of school before the break.

Einstein came into the room, barking happily. Dee picked him up and cuddled him. "I've been ignoring you for so long." She had been so wrapped up in the drama of all her problems that Joey had stepped in as the primary caregiver and entertainer for their cherished pet.

She kissed him, and he licked her neck. "I'm sorry, Einstein." She knew immediately that she was forgiven.

Einstein! Dee ran to her mother, Einstein in tow.

"Mom, what is Einstein going to do while we're away?" Dee felt panicked.

"Calm down, Dee. He's coming with us on the plane. We checked with the airline, and pets are welcome. We'll have to keep him in a pet carrier for the flight, but he'll be okay. The hotel is pet-friendly, too."

"Won't Florida be too hot for him? Look at all this black fur!" Dee thought she just might have an angle that would save the day and stop the move from occurring.

"The plane and hotel rooms are air-conditioned, so don't worry about that. He'll be fine." Mrs. Lanson hugged her daughter.

Dee retreated. Entering her room, she closed the door. She sat cuddling Einstein, who was content to be the recipient of her affection.

There were so many thoughts going through her

mind. It seemed that for every problem she had solved, she ended up with a new one to replace it. She knew that there were certain things she couldn't change: the move, and—she had discovered—the actions and reactions of others.

The Andrew problem irked her. It was unfortunate that he had seen the list she wrote about the many ways he bugged her. Then he had done the same back to her. To be fair, she had to admit that she kind of had it coming. Even though he was never intended to see that list, he had been hurt by it. Still, she couldn't help being angry. His note did hurt her, too, although she wasn't sure why.

That night at supper, the family discussed the plans for their trip. They were leaving the next day. Mrs. Lanson had taken charge of the packing, and Mr. Lanson had made all the arrangements for the flight, hotel, and rental car. The big topic was how it would feel to be in Florida for Christmas.

"It'll be so hot. It won't feel like Christmas at all," Dee whined.

"We were thinking," Mr. Lanson began, "that we should open one gift each while down there. Then, we can open the rest of the presents when we get home."

"Cool," exclaimed Joey. "It'll be like having two Christmases!" Even Dee liked the sound of that.

After supper, she scurried up to her room to call Sue and Samantha and tell them about the latest development with Andrew. They were surprised, as she knew they would be.

Tomorrow, she would be in Florida with her family. She enjoyed vacations, but was unsure how she felt about this one. After all, this trip would determine whether or not they would end up moving there. Dee tried not to think about that part of it when a vacation away from Andrew was in her future!

CHAPTER TWELVE

THE SCHEMING BEGINS

The departure day had arrived. Dee was excited about the trip, although she would not disclose this to her parents, who might take it as a sign that she wanted to move.

The plane ride was uneventful, except for some turbulence that worried her. Joey, on the other hand, would put both arms up into the air when the flight became bumpy and call out, "Weeeee!" Dee was glad someone could find enjoyment in the feeling that the plane wasn't running right. She looked at her parents, who were not disturbed in the least.

"Don't worry, Dee. The plane sometimes hits air pockets, which make the ride bumpy." Mrs. Lanson rubbed Dee's arm gently.

"Thanks." Dee hoped that Einstein was doing all right in the pet carrier.

Once on the ground, they left the airport and headed

for the rental car area. Dee noticed how hot it had become. *Feeling less excited....*

The hotel was their first stop. Mr. Lanson's company had put them up in a nice place. Feeling exhausted from travel, they decided to go out to eat and then return to the hotel to make plans for the following days.

Joey was a little antsy from being cooped up in the plane and rental car; he could hardly sit still in the restaurant.

"Joey, stop! You're driving me crazy with all that up-and-down you're doing." Dee was a bit edgy and low on patience.

In an effort to prevent the bickering that was likely to follow, Mr. Lanson suggested they play some word games. "I'll go first. I'm thinking of a word or phrase that will brighten everyone's spirits. What am I thinking of?"

"Sleep?" Mrs. Lanson guessed.

"Nope."

Dee looked at her father as she tried to figure out what he would consider happy. "Silly story?" Mr. Lanson was well-known for his creativity.

"Nope."

"I know!" Joey exclaimed as he jumped up out of his seat. "Time travel!"

"Now, Joey, that is an awesome guess, but I wouldn't know how to deliver on it!"

That reminded Dee of a conversation she and Joey had started months before. "Joey, you might not remember this, but just before school started, you told me that you had a cool idea of where you'd like to go in a time machine. Where were you thinking of going?"

Joey thought for a while. "Oh, yeah! I was thinking of

going into the future and being on the first expedition to Mars. That'd be the best!"

"I heard that the people on that mission wouldn't come back to Earth. They'd be stuck on Mars! What if you hated it?" Dee challenged.

"Then I'd get back in the time machine and come home! What do ya think?" Everyone laughed.

After a few more rounds of Mr. Lanson's game, no one had guessed what he was thinking of. "Are you ready for the phrase that will bring a smile to everyone's face and make me the hero of the day?" He stopped and said not a word.

"Dad…" Joey whined. "What is it?"

"Yes, we're ready!" Dee poked Joey in the arm for whining.

"DISNEY WORLD!" Mr. Lanson exclaimed.

That certainly brightened up the moment. Everyone started talking at the same time, excitedly interrupting each other. The volume at their table was on the rise, so the parents wisely decided it was time to go back to the hotel and plan.

"Which park will we go to?" Dee asked.

"Whichever one will make us happy!" Mr. Lanson made the rounds and hugged each family member.

"Don't forget to hug Einstein!" Dee picked up the dog and handed him to her father. Einstein seemed pleased to be included in the hugs.

The happiness faded as the rest of the vacation was outlined. "First, we need to check out the area we'll be moving to." That brought groans from Dee and Joey. "I'll show you the building where I'll be working." More groans. "We'll see what kinds of fun things there are in the town, too. We'll do this part of the vacation first so that we can spend the most time at Disney World."

"Yay!" they chorused at the last part of the plan.

"How far away is this town?" Dee asked.

"We're already here!" Mrs. Lanson announced. "Let's work out a rough schedule, and then get a good night's sleep."

The next day the excitement had plummeted, and Dee and Joey were dragging their feet. Neither was interested in exploring the town that would become their home, away from friends and all that was familiar to them.

During the grand tour, they saw the office building where Mr. Lanson would be working and the schools they would be attending. They drove through some nice neighborhoods where homes were up for sale. In one neighborhood, they saw lots of kids playing in a cul-de-sac at the end of a pretty long street. The homes were about the same size as the one they would be leaving behind. Mr. and Mrs. Lanson seemed very excited about the two homes for sale on this street and decided to check them out again the next day.

It was starting to feel like the move was definitely a done deal as they checked out possible houses to live in. Dee's dream of a different outcome looked bleak. She realized that when her parents had made the announcement, they did say the family *would* be moving to Florida. Yet, Dee couldn't help hoping for a way out.

As the tour continued, they saw that there were many beaches and nice parks. The next town over had a zoo and a very large mall. In spite of the nice area and the attractions they had discovered, Dee and Joey remained very quiet for the entire day.

They all went to see the two favorite houses the next day. The homes were so similar in structure and design that there was no definite preference between them. That night was Christmas Eve, and they went to church in the town where they would be living. Dee, looking around for kids about her age, was so preoccupied that it was difficult to focus on the service.

Dee and Joey had a secret meeting that night in their hotel room. "What do you think of all this?" Dee whispered.

Joey sighed. "I don't want to live here. Do you?"

"No, but what can we do about it?"

A smile came across Joey's face. "Well, Dad said we'd be in on every step of the plan. Let's vote no."

"Duh, obviously! But then it would be two against two. We'd still lose. Unless... we get Mom on our side!" Dee schemed.

"How can we do that? She'll always vote with Dad."

Dee leaned over and whispered her plan to Joey.

He giggled. "Excellent! I like it!"

* * *

Christmas Day was certainly different in Florida. The weather was sunny and 85 degrees. No snow. No fire in the fireplace. And in their case, no Christmas tree, stockings, or decorations. There would be the one present, but still. It was strange.

They returned to the same church for morning services. Back at the hotel, they received their one gift—a book about Florida. Dee and Joey exchanged knowing glances. This would be harder to reverse than they had thought, but Dee would try anyway. What did she have to lose?

They then went to a beach, and Dee and Joey built a sand castle—another odd thing to do on Christmas. After a while, Mrs. Lanson suggested that they all go for a walk along the water. While they were walking, Dee dropped back, away from the others.

"Come on, Dee! Keep up!" Joey yelled, louder than he needed to.

"I can't. It's too hot. I feel sick." Dee collapsed to her knees.

Mrs. Lanson ran to her. "What's the matter?"

"It's too hot. I don't feel good. I want to go home," she pleaded. "I feel sick." She looked up at her mother to see if she was buying it.

Mrs. Lanson put her hand on Dee's forehead and told her to look up. "Are you really sick? Tell the truth."

Dee had never been very good at lying, and she knew that her mother was well aware of this.

"Dee?"

"Yes, I'm s—" Dee's eyes met her mother's disbelieving gaze. "Well, I'm—not sick." She had no choice but to admit it. Her mother knew her all too well. "It's just that I don't want to move here. And Joey doesn't want to move, either. I don't want to leave my friends, and neither does Joey. Please, Mom!" The tears were now flowing. Dee wondered if there was more water coming out of her eyes than there was in the ocean in front of them.

"I don't know what to say, except that we need to do it, for Dad's sake," Mrs. Lanson said gently.

Joey came over to join them, and Dee tried to get his attention to put a halt to what she knew was coming, but he didn't notice. He collapsed dramatically on the sand. "Mom, this heat's making me so sick! I think I'm going to..."

Mrs. Lanson shook her head. "I know what you're doing. Dee tried the same thing."

Now Joey joined in the cry-fest. "But, I don't want to move here. Please don't make us!"

Mr. Lanson joined the others and sat on the sand with them. "I know this will be hard on you and on all of us, but we will adjust to it. You'll see."

"This is the worst Christmas ever!" Dee lamented.

"It's so unfair!" Joey chimed in. The only sounds that could be heard, besides the crashing waves, were the loud sobs of the two saddest kids in Florida.

After Dee and Joey went to bed, Mr. and Mrs. Lanson sat together. They had had a feeling that there would be some upset, but they were not expecting it to be this dramatic. They sat in silence for a long time.

"I'm sorry, Joe," Mrs. Lanson sighed. "This must be so hard on you."

He sighed as well. "To tell you the truth, I don't want to move either. We have a beautiful home now, in a nice neighborhood. The kids are settled into their schools. We all have great friends. If I quit my job to stay, I'll not likely find another job that pays as well. You know I looked for another job when the company first told us we would be relocating. There were no good jobs in our area."

Mrs. Lanson looked at him sympathetically. "I'd rather not move, but we must be realistic. You need to work. You've worked your way up in the company, and I don't think you'll be able to match your salary anywhere else if you have to start over. Children adjust, sometimes better than their parents, to things like this. We'll all be fine. Dee and Joey will make new friends and might discover that they like Florida better than home."

"I hope you're right. It's really bothering me to see how sad they are. I wouldn't hurt them for the world." He hung his head in sadness.

"Let's try to put a positive spin on the day. It's Christmas, after all. How about we plan the fun part of the trip?"

"Sounds like the best idea either of us has had all day!"

CHAPTER THIRTEEN

ANIMALS SMALL AND BIG

The next day, the family went to a local zoo and enjoyed seeing some of the tropical animals on display. Dee couldn't break herself away from the colorful birds. There were green parrots, red-and-green parrots, blue-and-gold macaws, and an all-white umbrella cockatoo, all posed on their perches and ready to delight.

Visitors could pay to have their pictures taken while holding a bird on their outstretched arm. Dee had fun watching one visitor after another posing with the birds.

"Would you like to hold one?" the attendant asked.

"Could I?" Dee looked at her parents for confirmation that this was okay. They nodded.

Dee selected the white umbrella cockatoo because it seemed to be the tamest bird. She paid the money and stretched her arm out. Joey stepped up to take the picture. All of a sudden, the bird scampered up Dee's arm and nestled its head into her hair, tangling a few strands in the process! *Click, click* went the camera.

She shook her head to get the bird to stop, but it likely thought she was playing, and it continued rubbing its head against hers. *Click, click.* By the time the attendant stepped in to remove the bird, Dee's hair was a matted mess. *Click, click.*

"This is excellent!" screeched Joey. He showed the camera around so the others could see the funny photos. Even Dee had to laugh. "I want to hold one now!" Joey declared.

Dee and Joey exchanged places. Dee took out her own camera, hoping to capture some crazy photos of Joey's encounter. He chose the active blue-and-gold macaw. Dee was ready.

The bird sat on Joey's arm and did not budge! Joey jiggled his arm a little to see if he could entice the bird to move up his arm but to no avail. Dee took a picture, which came out cute but not funny. She decided to find a way to pull a prank on her brother and get even.

Joey ran ahead. "Come on!" he called back over his shoulder. Dee hurried to catch up, with their parents right behind.

Another photo opportunity was presenting itself. This time, one could hold a four-foot baby alligator! Joey got in line.

The trainer was talking to a small group that had gathered. "You'll notice that the alligator's mouth is taped closed. That's because the baby alligator could bite someone's hand off."

"Cool!" Joey squealed. "This is the coolest thing ever!"

"Joey, no! You don't want to do this!" Dee cautioned him. "Mom? Dad?"

Mr. Lanson patted Dee on the shoulder. "He'll be fine.

The trainer is standing very close. Don't worry." He paid the attendant for the photo-op.

Dee, trying not to imagine her brother with one hand missing, offered to take the picture. Soon it was his turn, and he reached out his arms as the trainer helped to position the alligator. *Click.* The alligator was very tame and didn't move at all. Dee was glad that her brother had escaped peril. Then it happened.

"Dee, your turn!" Joey dared her.

Not wanting to be upstaged by her brother, but terrified at the same time, she stepped up to show him how brave she was. With her heart beating wildly, she reached out for the alligator, while Joey zoomed in with the camera to capture the moment. Dee wasn't sure she had one of her hands positioned correctly, so she tried to shift it just slightly. The alligator turned its head to look at her. *Click. Click.*

Full of anxiety, Dee went to give the alligator back to the trainer, but she had turned her back and was talking to the next group of visitors. *Click, click.* "Excuse me!" Dee called to the trainer. *Click. Click.*

"Oh, sorry! Don't worry; the alligator won't hurt you. As I mentioned, the mouth is taped shut." With that, she took the alligator and placed it into the arms of another eager child.

Joey was, once again, showing the pictures around. This time Dee wasn't laughing. She had been very fearful, wondering if the tape would hold, yet she had done it. *I can't believe I did that!*

The rest of the visit was filled with long walks along trails, more exhibits, and animal shows. Dee and Joey liked the bird show. One bird pedaled a tiny tricycle, and another rode a tiny scooter!

After a full day, they went out for supper and back to the hotel.

"Kids, we need to be up early tomorrow because we're going to Disney World!" Mr. Lanson announced. "Let's all pack tonight so that we can be ready at 5:30 AM for the long ride."

If his intention was to settle his children, he failed miserably. Dee and Joey were wild with excitement; they couldn't quiet themselves, or pack for that matter. Tomorrow, they were going to Disney World!

* * *

The car ride seemed long, and Dee and Joey were feeling restless.

"How much longer?" Dee whined after staring out the window for what seemed like forever. "This is boring!"

"This is taking too long," Joey complained.

Dee had an idea. "Dad, if I had a smartphone, then I'd never complain about a car ride. Can I get one?"

"I want one, too!" Joey chimed in.

"That would not solve your current problem, so let's focus on this car ride. How about this? Mom and I will take turns coming up with things for you to look for while we drive. The two of you can compete to see who spots the things first." Mr. Lanson hoped the game would keep them occupied for the duration of the trip.

The backseat passengers agreed to the plan.

"Okay. Red car," Mrs. Lanson called.

Two seconds later... "There!" Dee and Joey shouted at nearly the same time.

"I saw it first!" Dee said. "No, I did," Joey argued. Their parents exchanged frustrated looks.

"How about a blue car with Ohio license plates?" Mr. Lanson suggested. That was sure to take a while.

Five minutes later, a blue car with Ohio plates passed them. Joey spotted it first.

"I don't want to play anymore," Dee said. She took out a book and began to read silently. Joey wanted to continue the game, so Mr. and Mrs. Lanson took turns suggesting things to look for.

Finally they arrived, checked into their new hotel, and then headed out on their exciting adventure!

The first attraction was Animal Kingdom. After seeing some of the smaller animals at the local zoo, they decided to focus on the larger animals here. They boarded a vehicle to go out on a safari and see the African animals in modified versions of their natural habitats.

"Look at how long the necks are on those giraffes!" Dee called. "I wonder if they ever get neck pain from holding their heads up all the time."

"Whoa!" Joey stared in awe when they passed some lions. "I didn't know they'd be this big! Look at the head on that lion!"

"Look at how huge his paws are!" Dee exclaimed. "I'd be scared if I ever saw one of those when walking outside in the woods." The very thought of it sent shivers down her spine, and she got goosebumps on her arms. "That mane looks like it could use a comb. What do you think, Mom?"

"Shall I give him my hairstylist's card?" she quipped.

The elephants were another favorite among the group. Although the Lansons had seen them at a circus once or twice, it was better to see them in the modified habitat. Dee and Joey couldn't get over how big they were.

The next part of the tour would be the gorilla habitat. "I want to see the apes!" Dee called. "I learned in science class that our DNA is nearly the same as a chimpanzee's."

"I bet yours is *exactly the same* as a monkey's!" Joey teased. Then he began making annoying monkey noises. Dee ignored him.

When they arrived at the gorilla habitat, they didn't see any gorillas at first. Then, one with a baby gorilla on its back appeared from behind a large bush.

"Isn't that sweet?" Mrs. Lanson was impressed with the mothering instinct. They all were fascinated by the scenes before them.

"Africa is fun," Joey said, "but can we go to the dinosaur section next?"

"Hey, Joey—we could pretend we're going to the prehistoric era in a time machine!" Dee was ready to join her brother in mock time travel.

They headed for the exhibit and boarded a rover to go on a mission to save a dinosaur. The ride was thrilling and scary—with wild turns and dinosaurs popping out and roaring along the way! When the ride was over, Dee was pale.

"Are you all right, honey?" Mr. Lanson asked.

"That was terrifying!" Dee said. "I can safely say that if Joey ever makes a real time machine, I won't be going back to the dinosaur era!"

"That makes two of us! What a scary ride!" Mrs. Lanson was in total agreement with her daughter.

"Can we do it again, Dad?" Joey pleaded.

Mr. Lanson ruffled his hair and decided to join him for

a second pass through terror. He glanced over his shoulder at Dee and crossed his fingers while he made a "praying" motion. Dee laughed.

As Joey boarded the rover, Dee smiled as she remembered the time the previous summer when he climbed into the contractor's backhoe truck and was stuck in there all night. He was a character, all right!

Joey wanted to go to the park's make-believe dig site next. Dee found it too childish and assigned herself the job of photographer. She took some pictures and pleaded with her parents to move on.

They walked for what seemed like miles, looking at all the wonderful exhibits. Once fatigue set in and whining began, their parents suggested that they eat some supper and return to the hotel. Everyone slept well that night and arose eager to see what excitement the new day would bring.

CHAPTER FOURTEEN

PRANK REVENGE

EPCOT was next on the adventure tour. Dee noticed that EPCOT had a more intellectual tone to it. She liked that very much, especially the journey through America's history. There was another ride through time showing how human communication advanced and impacted the future. Joey was perhaps having the most fun in "time machines" that were not cardboard boxes!

Mr. and Mrs. Lanson enjoyed walking through an area that featured food and souvenirs from many different countries. The weather was unseasonably hot and humid for a December day. Dee had a hard time keeping up with everyone.

"Mom, I don't feel well," she wailed.

"Faker!" Joey called. "You tried it before. It won't work."

"Mom, I mean it!" Dee gasped, as if short of breath. That got her mother's attention.

"Dee, what is it? What's wrong?"

"I'm so hot. I feel sick. I have a headache, and I'm *not* faking it." Dee glared at her brother.

Mr. Lanson knelt down. "If you can hang on for a couple minutes, I'll lead you to a place where you can cool off and have something to drink. Can you make it?"

"I think so." Dee's tone was not convincing, so they departed immediately.

They reached a building in which visitors could sample sodas from around the world. Mrs. Lanson dashed over to the self-serve dispensers and poured Dee a cup of the first one she saw.

Dee sipped it, and her eyes nearly bugged out of her head. Swallowing hard, she hollered, "Augh! That's horrible! I think I'm going to be sick!"

Mrs. Lanson grabbed the cup from her, dumped the remaining liquid into a trash can, and then filled the cup with a different choice.

"This one's better!" Dee gulped it down and took some more. Her recovery was quick.

Joey finally made his way to the beverages, and Dee knew just what to do. "Joey, try this one. It's so delicious! You'll love it!" She filled the little cup to the rim and gave it to him.

"Gross!" Joey gasped and coughed. "That wasn't nice! You're mean!" He began wiping his tongue with his not-so-clean-looking hand.

"I dare you to drink the entire cup of it," Dee challenged him. "I bet you can't do it!"

"I *can!*" Joey declared. "Watch me!" With that, he pinched his nose and guzzled the entire amount of the bitter-tasting soda. *Click. Click.* She was proud of herself for capturing the scene in a photo. His face had turned a little green, which sent Dee into a round of hysterical laughter.

"You're brave; I'll give you that!" Dee put her arm around Joey. "Here," she said after filling a cup with a different soda choice. "You'll like this one." And he did. Dee had had her revenge. There was no need to prolong it.

Before any further mischief could take place, their parents led them back out into the heat to go back to the hotel.

Dee reflected that it had been a great couple of days. She loved to go to different places and learn new things. For the past two days, she had not given the move a thought. It was a pleasant break. Soon, though, she would be back at home and hear the verdict on whether she would lose all that she wished so desperately to hold on to. If her parents decided to uproot the family to Florida, how would she bear it?

* * *

When they entered their house after their vacation, Dee and Joey were delighted. The Christmas tree was a pleasant reminder that they had something special to look forward to. Their parents decided that the delayed celebration would take place the next day, when everyone would be well-rested. They all unpacked and settled in.

"Who would like to have pizza for supper?" Mrs. Lanson asked.

"I would!" the rest of the family replied in unison. And so, it was settled.

It was a quiet mealtime at first. Dee and Joey were afraid to talk about Florida and bring on the conversation about moving.

Mr. Lanson broke the ice. "What was your favorite part of our vacation?"

"Watching the bird mess up Dee's hair," Joey offered. "That was awesome!"

Dee shook her head at her brother. "I liked watching Joey's face when he drank that yucky soda. That was excellent!"

"Eileen, maybe we should have stayed home and saved the money. We took you kids to *Disney World*! Are you kidding me?" Mr. Lanson threw his hands up into the air in mock frustration.

"Just kidding, Dad. I liked the safari the best, I think— even if the size of the animals scared me!" Dee grabbed another slice of pizza.

"Not me!" Joey exclaimed. "I liked that dinosaur ride with all the scary dinosaurs jumping out at us. That was the coolest thing ever!"

Dee hoped her next question wouldn't lead to the conversation she and Joey wanted to avoid. "What did you guys like the best?"

"I'm with Joey on the dinosaur ride," Mr. Lanson said. "It was very intense. The second time was a little easier because we knew what to expect. It does make me think about what it would have been like to live back then, when dinosaurs roamed the Earth."

"Dad, I don't think you'd be around for very long." Dee giggled.

"Yeah, some T-Rex might get you before you had a chance to even look around!" Joey grabbed the last slice of pizza and stuffed half of it into his mouth. Dee groaned and looked away.

"My favorite part was sampling the foods from the different countries." Mrs. Lanson enjoyed cooking, and she had bought a cookbook that had recipes from the different countries represented in EPCOT.

Everyone had finished eating, so Dee and Joey made their escape to call their friends. Dee grabbed the phone first and called Samantha.

"Are you going to move there?" Samantha asked hesitantly.

"Probably, but they haven't told us for sure yet. It was so hot there, and it's only December! I almost fainted one day. Anyway, I hope Mom and Dad are still thinking about it." Dee sighed, trying to hold on to some hope.

"Don't panic yet," Samantha advised her. "Wait! You almost fainted? For real?"

Dee told her the whole story, and they shared a good laugh over the Joey incident. Samantha was a good and fun friend. It was hard for Dee to imagine that she and Samantha had once been enemies. She was glad that was behind them now.

Joey wanted the phone to call Samuel, and then it was Dee's turn again.

"Hey, Sue, it's Dee. I'm back!"

"You've got the wrong number. It's not Sue, it's Ronnie."

Dee gasped. "I'm sorry!" It was all she could come up with.

"Well, try again. Bye."

That was awkward! I guess she really doesn't want to be friends. The separation still hurt. Dee wished that they could be somewhat friendly, at least.

She then called Sue's number, correctly this time. Sue was relieved that there wasn't any bad news, yet.

The next day the Lansons had their belated Christmas

celebration. They opened gifts and had a special meal. While in Florida, they had already gone to church services, so it didn't seem like Christmas at all.

New Year's was in a couple of days. Dee wondered what the next year would hold. Would they stay, or would they go? Soon, all would be revealed.

CHAPTER FIFTEEN

FINAL DECISION

The Lansons awoke the next morning and found that a major snowstorm had taken out the power lines. Without electricity, there was no heat or light. The house felt cold. Very cold.

Joey knocked on Dee's door.

"What?" she called from the other side.

Joey then bounded into her room, uninvited. "Did you see all the snow outside? There must be three feet of snow on the driveway! Come look!"

Dee couldn't resist; she got out of bed and went to the window. "Whoa! I've never seen this much snow! Too bad it's not a school day. School would be canceled for a storm like this."

"Yeah." Joey looked at Dee with a sad expression on his face. "There'll be no snow in Florida. And, no snow days."

Dee put her arm around her brother's shoulder. "Yup,

that's right. No snow days there." She grabbed the comforter off the bed and wrapped it around herself and Joey as they sat together on the floor.

They exchanged stories of the most memorable snowstorms they had lived through. Joey once had built a snow fort and pretended it was a time machine. Mr. Lanson enjoyed making snow sculptures. Once, he sculpted a figure of George Washington out of snow, but some neighborhood kids destroyed it, and the Lansons never found out who was responsible. It had been a very good likeness, too.

"Do you think they've decided yet?" Joey whispered.

Dee took a deep breath. "I'm trying not to think about it. You don't want to go, do you?"

"No way! Do you?"

Dee shook her head. "They'll probably tell us soon, but I think we both know what their answer will be."

Just then, their parents knocked on Dee's door. "May we join you?" Mrs. Lanson asked.

"Sure. Grab a corner of the comforter if you want to be warm," Dee replied. She hoped that if she were extra nice, then the news would be good and not bad.

"There's a lot of snow out there," Mr. Lanson began. "We'll have shoveling to do later on."

The room went silent.

"Your father and I have come to a decision," Mrs. Lanson began. She took a deep breath and spoke softly. "We will be moving to Florida during your February vacation from school. We'll put this house up for sale in the meantime. We put a bid on a house in that cul-de-sac, and we'll know soon if our offer was accepted."

Dee and Joey sat, uttering not a word. Both seemed to

be frozen like ice and in complete shock.

Mr. Lanson cleared his throat. "We feel that this is the best thing for our family. It will be hard on all of us, but we are the Lansons, and we can get through anything. Who knows—it might even be fun!"

Neither Dee nor Joey offered any comment, but their facial expressions said it all. It was the saddest scene their parents had ever witnessed.

"Would you like to talk about it?" Mrs. Lanson asked gently.

Before either could answer, lights went on and the furnace rumbled to life.

"Well, that's a hopeful sign!" Mr. Lanson declared. "How about I make some of my famous pancakes to celebrate?" He stood up and stretched his legs.

"Just don't serve me that yucky drink from EPCOT!" Joey said.

At this point, Dee jumped up and did something totally unexpected. Stepping over the comforter, she gave her father a long hug. She wiped her tears with his shirt.

"Dee, it will be all right. We'll help one another. Speaking of helping, would you help me make the pancakes?"

"Okay," she said meekly.

And there it is: the news of dread. What can be done? Nothing. Nothing but wait and see how it all turns out.

CHAPTER SIXTEEN

AN UNLIKELY VOLUNTEER

New Year's Eve and New Year's Day were quiet at the Lanson home. Energy and spirits were low all the way around. For the entire family, the move to Florida would be a huge transition. Each family member was quiet, as if trying to process all that had to be done and what would change.

The return to school was going to challenge Dee in ways she couldn't have imagined. The first day back was clear, with no snow in the forecast.

"Well?" Samantha asked Dee at the very instant they saw each other. Samantha didn't even have to finish the question. Dee knew what she meant.

Dee avoided making eye contact. "Yup, we're moving."

"Oh," Samantha said.

The bell rang, and it was time for homeroom. The two went their separate ways. They would see each other again during third period, in gym.

English class was first, and Dee grabbed Sue's arm afterward. "We're moving." Before Sue could respond, Dee hurried away to get to her next class. She had planned it this way to avoid breaking into tears.

Dee and Samantha avoided the dreaded topic during gym class. At lunch, Dee's friends tried to cheer her up.

"We're going to spend summers together, don't forget," Samantha reminded her.

"We'll do it every summer!" Sue exclaimed.

"That's the only way I'm going to get through this," Dee said.

Andrew walked by their table and gave Dee a nasty look. Everyone noticed it. "Well, I guess there's one reason why moving away will be a good thing!" Dee shook her head.

At that, Andrew spun around and walked directly over to Dee. "What'd you say?"

Sue answered for her. "She said that one good reason for moving away was to get away from you!"

"You're moving?" Andrew looked confused.

"Yes."

"Why?" he pressed.

"Why do you care?" Samantha glared at him. "You're always so mean to her."

"Far away?" he continued, ignoring Samantha's commentary.

"Yes," Dee said again.

The bell rang, which ended lunch and the conversation. Andrew hurried away, tripped over a chair someone had forgotten to push in, and fell hard on his right wrist. Dee saw him yelp in pain but thought he was faking it.

History was next on the schedule, and Andrew did

not appear. Dee wondered if he was making his fall into a drama to avoid coming to class.

When Dee returned home from school, she had a surprise visitor.

"Penny!" she exclaimed. "Am I happy to see you!"

"Samantha's mom called and told me that you're going to move away. I thought you might need a friend. Are you okay?"

Dee's eyes filled with tears. "No, but Dad's company is moving there. If we don't go, he'll lose his job."

"Parents do need to work," Penny said gently. "However, we can't help feeling sad when things like this happen."

"I don't want to go. This is so hard. I'll lose all my friends."

"Well, you won't lose the other two in the Trendy Trio. You three are solid! And," Penny smiled as she continued, "you're stuck with me, too. I have every intention of writing to you. Maybe, if you invite me, I'll even come to visit."

"Yes, you must come! That would help me to feel better. Honestly."

"That isn't the only reason I came here today. When I found out which town you're moving to, I laughed. I have a cousin who lives there! She's Joey's age, and her name is Anika."

"Really? Do you ever visit your cousin?"

"Yes. Twice a year: July and December."

"Will you come to visit me when you go there?"

"You bet I will!"

Suddenly, Dee had a ray of hope shining into her dark corner. Maybe there was a chance for a happy outcome after all.

* * *

The next day, Andrew appeared in History class with a cast on his arm and hand. Apparently, he hadn't been faking after all. Mr. Chu was showing a PowerPoint presentation and encouraged everyone to take notes.

Andrew raised his casted hand. "I can't write with this cast on."

"Is there anyone who would be willing to copy over notes for Andrew?" the teacher inquired.

At first, no one offered. Then an unlikely hand was raised. "I'll do it, Mr. Chu," Dee said.

Andrew looked over at her with surprise, if not shock.

Dee wasn't sure why she had done it. He teased her mercilessly. Maybe she felt a little responsible for his accident; he had been hurrying away from their conversation when he tripped and fell. There was also something different about him in that conversation. He had acted almost disappointed with the news that she would be moving....

"Thank you, Delores," Mr. Chu said.

When Dee looked over at Andrew again, he gave her a casted thumbs-up. She couldn't help but smile at the irony of it. After all, she would soon be free of him, so what did it matter?

At home, she worked hard to copy over her notes. She did this before starting her homework. *What's happening to me? I've got things all mixed up! Me, helping Andrew? Yikes! Maybe I do need to get away from here!*

The next day, she stood outside Andrew's homeroom so that she could deliver the goods. When he arrived, he walked right by her and went into the room, where he joined a group of friends.

Dee marched in right after him. "Here, Andrew. These are the notes from yesterday."

He grabbed them and stuffed them carelessly into his backpack. "Thanks." He then turned away and resumed talking and laughing with his friends. With an eye-roll, Dee left and went to her own homeroom.

In each class, the teachers asked for volunteers to write notes for Andrew. As usual, there were no other volunteers, so Dee found herself doing it. He was no more thankful with each passing day. She found herself growing weary of the task, but she didn't regret it. During these weeks, she had been free of his teasing.

By the beginning of February, Andrew's cast had been removed and was replaced with a splint. "Hey, Dee!" he called before their Social Studies class started.

She turned and noticed the splint. "Can you write now?" She had her fingers crossed.

"Yeah, but I don't want to." He had a funny smirk on his face. "It's just that I got A's on my tests when I studied from your notes. So, if you wouldn't mind..."

"Yes, I do mind!" Dee exclaimed. However, she was pleased to hear the positive feedback about his grades as the result of her efforts.

"You can't blame a guy for trying!"

Just then, Mr. Chu entered the room, and all the students scrambled to their seats.

Dee was pleased to be relieved of the extra responsibility of copying over all of her notes in three classes. She wondered if the teasing would resume.

It had all been a distraction from the reality that faced her every time she went home. Realtors came with prospective buyers to look at the house several times a week.

Mrs. Lanson expected Dee and Joey to help keep things neat and orderly so the house would look its best. This was not an easy task when they were continually packing things away in boxes for the movers.

Dee and Joey went out with friends as often as possible. It was better to be away from home at this time. The move was only two weeks away.

CHAPTER SEVENTEEN

SAYING GOODBYE

The last day of school before February vacation had arrived. The students were more unsettled than usual; teachers had a harder time restoring order in their classrooms. Dee had awoken with a headache, so the chaos was not appreciated. Her melancholy mood was, in part, due to having to say goodbye to her friends.

All day, Dee stared at the clock. The minutes seemed to feel more like hours. She couldn't wait for the day to end, to get the inevitable over with. Seeing her friends in class stressed her out. Luckily, there wasn't much chance to socialize then. Lunch, on the other hand, would be a different matter.

Dee got in line to buy a lunch and looked around for Samantha and Sue. They had not yet arrived, so Dee paid for her lunch and chose a table.

Suddenly, Andrew approached and sat down with her. "What's up?" he said.

"What are you doing here?" Dee was annoyed that he had chosen her table on her last day at this school.

"I was sent here," was his mysterious reply.

"Who sent you?" Dee was hoping it was Pete. She wondered if Andrew had told him about the move and then was supposed a deliver a message.

Andrew seemed quite settled at the table, and began to open his milk. His splinted hand made the maneuver awkward, and the milk splashed everywhere. Dee jumped up out of the way—but not quickly enough. There were milk splatters on her shirt and jeans.

"Sorry!" Andrew said, but he had gotten the worst of it.

Dee couldn't be angry with him; he was injured, after all. She scurried away to wash the milk off. The milk stain eventually disappeared, but now she was left with water spots on her clothes. She looked in the mirror and laughed at the sight.

Carrying her backpack to cover her wet front, she returned to her table. Andrew was nowhere to be found.

Sue approached Dee and pointed across the cafeteria. "We're over there. We didn't see you come in."

Dee removed the strategically placed backpack. "Oh!" Sue exclaimed. "What happened?"

As they crossed the cafeteria, Dee told the story. They had to walk around a group that was blocking the way to the table Sue had pointed out.

"Surprise!!!" Sue, Samantha, and several other classmates called out.

Dee was stunned and not sure what was going on at first. Suddenly, Andrew—with large wet spots on his own clothes—pushed through the crowd. "I told you I was sent. Sue asked me to distract you. I guess I did *too* good a job of it!" he added after noticing her wet clothing.

Sue sent Andrew to distract me? This was certainly a day full of surprises.

A few classmates gathered around to ask Dee about the move and tell her that she would be missed. Dee suddenly felt a little popular. She thought of times during the previous year when crowds gathered around Pete and made her jealous. It felt good to be on the other side for once.

Samantha brought in cupcakes that had gotten a little squished in transit, but were delicious just the same. Dee's headache disappeared, as did her anxiety about saying goodbye to her friends. Instead, this felt more like a celebration.

That evening, Mrs. Perry invited Dee and Sue to join herself and Samantha for ice cream and a little party at the mall. They sat down and studied the menu.

Midway through their sundaes, a group of boys walked in. There was a bit of commotion, which caused Dee to look over at them with annoyance. There sat Andrew, grinning from ear to ear! He waved his splinted hand. The boy sitting across from him turned around to see whom he was waving to.

Pete! Dee felt flustered and not sure how to react. So, she just waved. Pete was just as cute as ever. She could feel her face getting redder by the second.

Before long, Pete and Andrew came over to the table. After greeting Mrs. Perry politely, the boys said hi to the others.

"So, you're really going to move?" Andrew said to Dee. "I bet you just wanted to have a party, and we'll see you at school after vacation."

"Moving?" Pete asked. "Where are you going?"

"Florida," Dee managed to say.

"When?" Pete seemed quite surprised.

"We're leaving in two days." Dee sighed, suddenly not wanting to go at all.

"Well, have fun," Pete said. He started to turn away.

"Do you like your new school?" Dee asked.

"It took some getting used to, but it's all right, I guess."

"I'm not looking forward to going to a new school. I hope I don't hate it."

"Well, then, you could come back!" Andrew said cheerfully.

"Good luck, Dee. Nice seeing you all," Pete said, and then the boys went back to their table.

It amused her that she kept running into boys she knew at the mall or ice cream shop. *I guess we all love ice cream!*

She had experienced many adventures that day. Seeing Pete was, perhaps, a fitting end to her time in New England. She hoped that she would have a pleasant beginning in her new location. That, however, remained to be seen.

CHAPTER EIGHTEEN

ALONE AND LONELY

The move to Florida went smoothly. The unpacking took a long time, but by the end of February vacation, the Florida house was ready to be lived in.

The news from New England was not nearly so positive; their old house had not yet sold. Sandra, the realtor, recommended that they rent it out instead. After careful consideration, that's what Mr. and Mrs. Lanson decided to do. It wasn't ideal, but it seemed to be the best choice.

Dee and Joey were registered in their new schools, so they were all set to begin. Middle school included sixth grade in Florida as well, a fact Dee was happy about. She was anxious about how the first day would go but eager to get it over with. Would the other students accept her? Would she make friends?

The bus picked her up promptly at 7:40 AM. She found a seat easily but sat alone. She attracted a bit of attention from curious onlookers, yet no one spoke to her.

In homeroom, the teacher introduced her to the other students, but after an initial greeting, no further conversations occurred. It was the same in all the morning classes. Dee felt out of place and uncomfortable. She had hoped it would be different.

She sat alone at lunch until a heavyset girl with braces joined her. "Can I sit here?" she asked.

"Sure. I'm Dee. What's your name?"

"Marissa. I've never seen you before. Are you new here?"

"Yeah. My family just moved here. Today's my first day." Dee unwrapped her sandwich.

"Where did you used to live?" Marissa opened her carton of milk.

No spills, Dee noted. Not like the day with Andrew. "New England."

"Oh." Marissa took a bite of her pizza.

"What grade are you in?" Dee asked, hoping to make a friend.

"Sixth. You?"

"Also sixth. I hope we're in some classes together. You're the only one who has talked to me today." Dee hoped that didn't sound dumb.

"I'm not surprised. It can be kind of cliquey and hard to break into a group. I live here, and I'm still trying."

Dee felt a little sorry for her and didn't quite know what to say after that. She wanted to know more but was afraid to ask. They ate in silence for the rest of the lunch period.

The afternoon went along just like the morning. Marissa was the only student to talk to her all day.

Dee felt very lonely on the bus ride home. The seat

next to her remained empty for the duration of the ride. She wondered if Joey was having the same experience. She wouldn't have to wait long to find out.

At 3:30, Joey dashed into the kitchen. "Florida rocks! My new friend Dylan likes science, too. He thinks time travel will be real someday!"

Dee couldn't help but smile. Anyone interested in time travel would be a fast friend for him. "How did you find that out? You just met him!"

"Well, we did journal-writing, and we could read what we wrote to the class. When the teacher asked me if I wanted to share, I said okay. I wrote about time travel, and Dylan said he likes to think about it too."

Feeling a bit inspired, Dee tried to imagine some conversation starters for herself. It was tough being shy. Big groups intimidated her; she liked small groups or one person at a time. It was hard for her to break into a group, even when she had known the people for a long time.

Her group from home had started with only herself and Sue. Then Ronnie joined, and finally Samantha. Well, Ronnie was now out, but the point was that it was a gradual transition. *Maybe I should make a list of topics I could talk about.*

Conversation Starters

1. What do you like to do for fun? (Lame)

2. Have you ever been to New England? (Lamer)

3. What is your favorite TV show? Movie? (Maybe)

4. Do you have any sisters or brothers? (Lamest)

5. Do you like to read? (Maybe too geeky)

Remembering the disaster that occurred after her last list fell into the hands of Andrew, she crinkled up the paper. She still felt bad about hurting his feelings, even if he was a pest. When he got her back with his own hurtful "list," she had understood what it felt like.

She went to her room, plopped herself onto her bed, and stared at the ceiling. *How am I going to make friends? I'm the new kid. I feel like I must be invisible.* Then she thought about Marissa—the one person who had talked to her. That had been a bit awkward because the conversation had just died, and they ended up not talking for what seemed like a really long time. She might try again with Marissa, though. Maybe she was just shy also.

Dee took a deep breath. Suddenly, for the first time since the move, she really, really missed her old friends.

* * *

The next day, Joey was full of excitement about seeing his new friend at school. Dee was apprehensive about trying to even get a conversation started. She went to her wastebasket and took out her list. Unfolding the page, she studied it, desperately looking for something that would help her break the ice. She put the paper in her backpack.

No. Remembering the danger of having a personal list in one's backpack, she removed it again and returned it to the wastebasket.

The bus ride that morning had gone no better. *Alone again.* There was no time during her classes to talk with anyone, so she decided that she would try to find Marissa at lunch, but she was nowhere to be seen.

Dee sat at a table, hoping that someone would come to

join her. A group of girls did, but she didn't recognize any of them, and no one acknowledged her.

There was, however, a happy surprise waiting for her at home: two letters! She couldn't find a letter opener, so she ripped open the first envelope.

Hi Dee!

I hope you're having fun in your new school. English won't the same without you. Andrew might actually be quiet without having you to bug. LOL

Samantha's coming over next Friday, so we'll call you! Maybe we can make plans for the summer. That's weird because it's snowing here... again!

Hopefully, we'll have Ronnie news! Talk to you Friday! I can't wait to hear your updates!

Sue

Dee smiled for the first time all day. It was only Tuesday, but in three days she would talk with her friends! Up to this point, she had avoided calling them because things weren't going all that well in Florida. Maybe by Friday, the situation would be improved.

She ripped open the second envelope.

Hi Dee,

I hope all is well in Florida. Have you or Joey met my cousin Anika yet? You'll really like her. Her favorite subject is science, so tell Joey about

her. I think they should be in the same grade.

High school is going fine, but it's a lot of work.

Samantha is doing great. Oops, I probably should have left that bit of news for her to tell you herself. She misses you a lot.

If you feel like writing, I'd love to hear from you.

Take care,
Penny

It was nice to get snail mail from her friends. Dee really liked getting letters in the mail, so she hoped it would continue. Samantha had not yet written, but Dee guessed that she was busy. Dee had some homework to do, so she put the letters aside and began her science questions.

"Joey, have you met Anika?" she asked during suppertime.

"Yeah, she's in my class. She likes to talk to Dylan and I at recess."

"Dylan and *me*," Dee interrupted.

"Yeah, that," Joey said.

"Penny said that she likes science." Dee reached for a roll and some butter.

"Oh, yeah, she does!" Joey chuckled. "We might even invite her to play time travel with us. She also likes music and a bunch of other stuff." He reached for his glass of milk and drank more than half of it at once. "Hey, Dee, look at me! I'm old!" He turned to show her his white milk mustache.

"Joey, wipe that off! You look ridiculous!" Dee turned away from him.

"Geez, what a grouch," he said.

Dee realized that she was being mean, but she was jealous of how quickly he made friends, while she was still struggling to make even *one* friend.

She hoped that her luck would change. It certainly couldn't get much worse.

CHAPTER NINETEEN

THE WARNING

Here I am, on Day Three in my new school. It would be nice if I could make one friend. Not a hundred. Not ten. Just one. Is that too much to ask?

In science, Dee got paired with another student for an experiment. He had never spoken during discussions and seemed to have no friends, at least in science class. He was gawky in appearance, with braces on protruding front teeth.

Dee sat at the lab table on his left. "Hi, I'm Dee." She had decided to be the one to break the ice, instead of waiting for someone else to do it.

"Hi," came the quiet reply. The student kept his head down and made no eye contact.

"What's your name?"

"Jeremy." He never looked up, and the conversation died right there.

Well, I tried. However, Dee was still frustrated by his

lack of response. "I guess we should get started on the experiment."

While she was reading the directions, she noticed that Jeremy was already beginning the work. "What are you doing?" she inquired.

"The experiment."

"Did you read the directions?" Dee was afraid this would prove to be another lost-cause group project that would lower her grade. She took a deep breath and tried not to blow up.

"Yeah. I'm a fast reader. I like science," his voice dropped off, "a lot."

"Oh, okay." Dee finished reading the directions and looked over the work he had already done. *Wow! So far, so good!*

He spoke little, and only about the experiment. The lab report was due the next day. Dee looked at the questions they would be required to answer, and she was confident that they had received good data for their effort.

Soon, the bell rang, and the students moved to the next class.

At lunch, Dee looked for Marissa but didn't find her. Noticing Jeremy sitting alone, she took a seat at an empty table next to his. A group of girls sat down at her table but ignored her.

A group of boys, probably seventh-graders, walked up to Jeremy. "Hey, Bucky Beaver! What are you having for lunch? Bark? Grass?" They laughed and taunted him some more.

Dee couldn't believe her ears. *How cruel!* What bothered her was that Jeremy just sat there and didn't defend himself. She couldn't take her eyes off him.

"Excuse me, whoever you are," said one of the girls at her table. "Don't waste your time worrying about that loser." All the girls laughed. "He's a real weirdo."

Really? Dee was disgusted. She got up, took her tray, walked over to Jeremy's table, and sat down. "Hey!" she said cheerfully.

"You probably don't want to sit here if you value your reputation," Jeremy warned her. He turned away from her and continued eating his lunch.

"What's that supposed to mean?"

"You're new here, and sitting with me might not help you. I'm not very popular," Jeremy explained.

"Neither am I," Dee confessed. "I've been here three days, and no one has talked to me except one girl, who actually *stopped* talking to me after like a couple sentences. Anyway, why were those boys saying mean things to you?" She reached for her carton of milk and opened it very carefully.

"They always say things like that to me. I'm used to it."

"I was picked on by a boy in my old school," Dee offered.

"Oh," was his short reply. When she didn't continue with her story, he asked, "Why?"

"I don't know." Then Dee found herself going on and on about Andrew to Jeremy. It occurred to her that Jeremy had not offered any comment, and suddenly, she felt dumb. "Sorry," she muttered.

"I'm surprised you came over," he said, changing the subject. He turned to look at her, and she caught a glimpse of the other side of his face, which for some reason she had never seen before. She gasped, and her eyes grew wide in shock. The right side of Jeremy's face was deformed.

"I get that a lot," he told her.

Feeling totally embarrassed, Dee didn't know what to say. Finally, she managed, "I'm sorry... I didn't know."

"Well, now you do, so I'm guessing you'll move to a different table." He avoided making eye contact with her and ate some watermelon from his lunch tray.

Dee smiled. "Then you've guessed wrong. If it's okay, I'd like to stay here and finish my lunch."

It was Jeremy's turn to smile. "Sure."

The girl from Dee's table who had issued the warning walked over to her and whispered, "You should have taken my advice."

"What was that about?" Jeremy asked.

Dee hoped he hadn't heard what the girl said. "Nothing."

Just then, the bell rang. "Good luck with the lab report!" Dee called.

"You, too."

Dee was very confused. How could anyone be so cruel? Jeremy seemed nice and smart. He couldn't help having a deformed face or stick-out teeth. Even Andrew hadn't been *cruel* to her. The teasing was annoying, but he wasn't hateful, or at least she didn't think so.

Andrew. Why do I keep thinking of him? It was starting to occur to her that Andrew might not have been the beast she had made him out to be. He wasn't mean, or *really* mean like the boys she had seen earlier. Maybe he was just a boy—though an annoying one. Pete had never been like that, though, and he was a boy. Dee couldn't figure it out.

At home, she settled down to do her lab report. She was happy that Friday was approaching; she could talk with her friends! *Two more days!*

* * *

On Thursday, the day started out like all the others. Dee had never thought of herself as outgoing, but she did like to have friends. She was grateful that Jeremy was nice to her. She hoped that they would do more labs together.

Today wouldn't be the day for that, as the teacher showed a DVD on life science. It was interesting, but there was no time for talking with classmates. However, lunch would provide Dee with the opportunity she was hoping for.

She entered the cafeteria and spotted Jeremy, already seated alone, with his lunch tray in front of him. After buying her lunch, she approached him. "Hey, Jeremy! May I sit here?"

"There's probably no law against it," he said. Dee was confused by his answer and just stood there. He then looked up and added, "Just kidding! Of course, you can sit here."

"Well, if you don't want me to..."

"Sit!" Jeremy looked up again, and smiled this time.

"Don't tease me!" Dee laughed. "I had enough of that in my old school!"

The conversation picked up from there as they discussed the science program they had watched. They laughed when recalling a funny scene from the video.

Suddenly, a group of boys approached their table. Dee recognized them as the same ones from the day before.

"Hey, new girl," one said as he poked her arm. "This guy you're sitting with isn't worth it. You seem like a cool girl. Take a hint—find a new table."

Stunned into speechlessness, Dee froze. She wanted to tell the boys off, but no words would come out. The boys purposely bumped into Jeremy's arm as they went by him, while making their version of beaver noises.

Again, Jeremy did not react. He simply ignored them.

"Jeremy, why don't you tell them off?" Dee wondered the same thing about herself. She could have done it just as well as he.

"I don't care. Like I said yesterday, I'm used to it."

"They're wrong to be mean to you. Why can't people just be nice?"

"Don't worry about it."

Just then, the bell rang, and students scattered to their next classes.

Dee was bothered by the occurrence during lunch and couldn't get it out of her mind. The rest of the day seemed but a blur. She hopped onto the bus at the end of the day and went home.

Joey arrived home about 20 minutes later than usual, with Dylan and Anika right behind him. Mrs. Lanson looked a bit surprised, as Joey had not asked to have any-one over to the house.

Joey introduced his friends to his mother, and Mrs. Lanson smiled. "It's very nice to meet you both. Do your parents know that you're here?"

"Yeah," Joey interrupted. "Their bus stop is just before mine, so we went there first to check, and here we all are!" He went to the snack cabinet and got some cookies for the group.

"How did you get here, if not by bus?" Mrs. Lanson was confused.

"My mom drove us after Dylan asked his mother," Anika said.

Dylan looked up at Mrs. Lanson. "Joey said that you have lots of empty boxes."

"Yes, we have lots and lots of boxes from our move," she replied.

"Could we use one for a time machine?" Joey asked.

"Of course!" Mrs. Lanson left the room briefly and returned with one huge box, three flashlights, and some colorful markers. "I thought you might need these to make control panels."

"Joey, you have the coolest mom!" Anika exclaimed.

"Thank you. That is very sweet of you to say." Mrs. Lanson winked at Joey and whispered to him, "Don't you forget it!"

"You're way cool, Mom!" Joey exclaimed. "I already know it!"

The three third-graders worked hard on the time machine. The box was big, but a bit cramped when all three were inside. Dee heard them laughing and playing.

She was happy to know that Joey was settling into life in Florida. She recalled the day he ran away because he didn't want to move. Now he was adjusting well—in fact, better than she was. She was determined that her story would have a happy ending, too.

Once Dylan and Anika went home, Mr. and Mrs. Lanson called a family meeting.

"Joey, I'm glad that you have friends, but what happened today was very concerning," Mrs. Lanson began. "You got off at a bus stop that was not your own and rode in a car with someone we have never met."

"What's the big deal? Their mothers are nice," Joey protested.

Mr. Lanson spoke up. "We're new here; all people are strangers to us. You were lucky that these mothers were nice, but from now on, do not get into a car with anyone your mother and I have not met, and get off only at your own bus stop."

"Yeah, Joey, what were you thinking?" Dee added in her two cents' worth. "You need to use that noggin of yours for *something*."

"Hey, be nice!" Joey scolded her. Then, turning to his parents, he said, "Sorry."

The meeting was dismissed, and Dee went to her room and thought about her own predicament. Maybe it was time to step out of her shell and make something happen in her life. She was more than ready.

CHAPTER TWENTY

NEWS FROM HOME

Friday had finally arrived, and Dee couldn't have been happier. Tonight, she would talk to Sue and Samantha. How much she had missed them! She couldn't wait to hear the news from home—her old home, that is. Sue had written that there was Ronnie news. *What's that all about?*

The morning seemed to drag on longer than usual. Finally, it was time for lunch.

Dee and Jeremy ended up next to each other in the lunch line. He followed her to a table and began to ask, "May I..."

"Sit!" Dee exclaimed. She liked sitting with Jeremy. He was easy to talk to, and he was nice to her.

It wasn't long before the same group of boys made an appearance by their table. "Well, well, well," one of them said. "Two little lovebirds, together again."

Another piped up and said, "One little bird and one

beaver, that is!" With that, they all began making annoying beaver noises.

Dee remembered how Samantha had once come to her defense against Andrew, and she knew what she had to do. Standing up, she faced the boys. Actually, she was looking at their necks because they were so much taller than she. *Uh-oh...*

But she would not be intimidated. With her hands on her hips, she erupted, "Knock it off! You're not funny. You're mean—you're all a bunch of bullies. Leave Jeremy alone! He's really nice, but *you're* not. If anyone's a loser around here, just look in the mirror!"

One of the boys went to mock her by putting his hands on his hips and was about to say something, but Dee didn't give him a chance.

"And for your information, Jeremy is my friend! I sit here because I want to sit with him! So, JUST LEAVE US ALONE!"

All of a sudden, cheers could be heard from neighboring tables. "Way to go!" someone called out.

A cafeteria monitor made her way over to them, and the boys promptly left. "Is everything all right here?" she asked.

Dee sat down. "Yes," she said quietly. "Sorry."

"If they give you any more trouble, let me know." The monitor then walked away.

"Whoa." Jeremy appeared to be shocked. "That was nice of you, but you didn't have to do that for me."

"I hate mean people, and I've had enough of them. I hate bullies!"

Jeremy smiled a toothy smile. "So, we're friends?"

"Well, I wouldn't do that for an enemy, would I?" They

laughed at that thought.

Lunch was soon over, and on the way out of the cafeteria, a girl stopped Dee. "That was awesome, what you did back there. I'm Elena, by the way."

Dee nodded. "I'm Dee. Nice to meet you."

"Those jerks had it coming to them, but no one dared to tell them off. Until now!" Elena nodded her approval.

"I'm new here, so I hope I didn't make a mistake. Do you think they'll come after me?" For the first time, Dee realized that there might be consequences for her actions.

"I doubt it. They're a bunch of cowards, as well as jerks. Well, see ya. Gotta get to gym class. Nice job!"

"Thanks."

This day had turned out to be more epic than she had imagined. She had not just stepped out of her shell; she had blown up the shell! It was uncharacteristic of her... or *was* it? Suddenly, she recalled the time she exploded at Samantha when Samantha stared at her all the time and she didn't know why. How ironic was it that, afterwards, she and Samantha became the best of friends? She doubted that she would ever become best friends with any of those mean boys. That would be weird, if not impossible.

Later that evening, the phone rang, and Dee ran to answer it.

"Samantha!" she screeched. "I'm happy to hear your voice!"

"I'm here, too," Sue added.

"Cool! Tell me all your news!" Dee demanded. "I miss you two *so* much!"

"We miss you too," Samantha said. "Okay, I'll go first. I'm doing great in school, and I actually get the math!

Penny has really helped me. I even have a B in English!"

"That's awesome, Samantha! I knew you could do it! Sue mentioned that you might have Ronnie news. What's going on?"

It was Sue who took on this topic. "You won't believe this, but Ronnie cut her hair and colored the ends purple! She wears short skirts, too! Seriously, Dee, you wouldn't recognize her!"

"Why's she doing all that?" Dee asked.

"Who knows? She's really changed since last year," Sue said.

"And not for the better," Samantha added. "What's going on with you, Dee?"

"Where do I start? Well, Florida is getting hotter each week, which I hate. Joey's made some friends.... Ooh, Samantha—Joey met Anika, Penny's cousin! She came over the other day."

"Cool!" Samantha exclaimed. "What about you? Have you made any friends?"

Dee told the whole story of being lonely, then meeting Marissa, and finally meeting Jeremy. She explained how she told the boys off.

"Yikes, that's brave!" Sue commented.

"Well, I got my confidence from Samantha. She told off Andrew for me!"

"Yeah, but that was Andrew, not a group of older boys!" When Samantha said it that way, Dee realized how gutsy she had actually been.

They talked on and on, until Dee's mother finally put a stop to the call.

"I have to go too," Sue said. "Let's do this again soon!" After saying their goodbyes, they hung up.

Dee wished that she could go back to her old home and her own group of friends. She missed the Trendy Trio and was envious of Sue and Samantha, who could see each other any time they wanted.

She also thought about the Fantastic Four. *What is Ronnie up to?* Dee had been wondering about her former friend's behavior for months, but the report from Sue made her even more curious. *Well, it doesn't matter now.*

The weekend was here, and Dee decided to rest. At church, she prayed for friends. She left feeling better and hopeful that her luck was about to change.

CHAPTER TWENTY—ONE

NEW FRIENDS

Monday morning arrived and brought with it an unexpected rainstorm. Dee had noticed that when it rained in Florida, it often rained really hard. Then, sometimes it would stop abruptly, and the sun would come out.

The sun didn't appear to be anywhere in sight at the moment. Dee grabbed an umbrella and went out to wait for the bus, but the umbrella didn't do much good. Her jeans were soaked up to her knees. *Another reason to hate this place.*

The bus finally arrived, and Dee climbed up the steps.

"Sit here!" a voice called out, but Dee walked right on by. "Dee!"

With that, she turned around and saw that Elena was waving her over to sit next to her. "I didn't know we were on the same bus," Dee said as she settled into the seat.

"Until Friday, I didn't know who you were. Now everyone knows you! You're a hero for telling off those jerks.

Everyone was talking about it after lunch." Elena smiled.

"I don't feel like a hero. I'm scared those guys will be mean to *me* now."

"That would be bad!"

Dee was trying to think of some conversation starters that weren't lame, but she couldn't think of any. Finally, she asked, "Where do you live?"

"A few streets away."

"That's nice." *Lame! Why can't I think of anything better to say?*

It was quiet for a while. Then Elena spoke. "Do you have a brother named Joey?"

"Yes, how'd you know?"

"I'm Dylan's sister!"

Dee was so surprised that she could have been pushed over by a gentle breeze. She had not known that Dylan had a sister.

They compared notes on what it was like having a time-traveling younger brother. There were more than a few giggles coming from their seats! Once at school, they separated to go to homeroom.

After homeroom, Dee walked into English, her first class of the day. On the way to her desk, she saw someone waving.

"Elena! I didn't realize we were in English together!" Dee walked over to her.

"I just got bumped up to this level," Elena whispered. "My other classes were too easy. Here's my new schedule." She handed the paper to Dee. "Do we have any other classes together?"

Dee laughed out loud. "Elena, you're in all my classes—

even gym!" Despite the rain, she hoped that her luck had finally turned around.

The morning seemed to drag by. Dee looked out the window and watched the rain falling like sheets. She could hardly see anything through it.

Finally, the hour turned to 12, and the bell rang. Dee was late for lunch because she had stopped off in the girls' room first. Elena was sitting at one table in the cafeteria, and Jeremy was sitting alone at another. *Oh, no! What should I do?*

Jeremy looked up and smiled. Dee headed toward him but spotted Elena waving her over. Dee took a slight turn and walked toward Elena. Jeremy saw this, shook his head in despair, and stared down at his meal. Rejection. It was happening to him again.

"Hey ya!" a voice called out. Jeremy looked up to see Dee and Elena setting their trays down across from him!

"I heard there's probably not a law against it, so may we sit with you?" Dee sat down and met his eyes. She saw his face brighten.

"Sure. Even if there's a law against it, you could sit here anyway. If you want to..." His voice trailed off.

Dee crinkled up her napkin and threw it at him. "Duh! We want to sit with you, Jeremy!"

They talked about the upcoming science class. Then, Jeremy and Elena began talking about a nature show they had both seen on TV. Dee hadn't seen it, but she enjoyed watching her new friends talking about it.

New friends! All of a sudden, her hopes had come true. Not in the way she had expected, but there it was, right in front of her! Dee smiled to herself. Not only had she met two nice people, she had met two *really smart* nice people!

Maybe living in Florida was starting to grow on her. Except for the heat, those annoying boys, and missing her New England friends. However, it was a beginning, and that had to mean something. Right?

CHAPTER TWENTY-TWO

SPRING BREAK

Almost a month after the Lansons arrived in Florida, it was time for spring break. Students at this school in Florida had a different spring-break schedule than what Dee was used to. In her old hometown, there was a February vacation and an April vacation. In this school, there was only a March vacation, but classes ended much earlier in June. Dee enjoyed the February and April vacations, so she wasn't sure what to think of this schedule. Like every other new part of this transition, she would have to wait and see.

Dee's family had no vacation plans, which was fine with her; she had had enough excitement to last a very long time! She had taken some books out of the library and planned to read in her free time. That is, when Joey wasn't interrupting her train of thought, which was more often than she cared for.

"Guess what, Dee? Dylan and Anika are coming over today!"

"Where are you going this time? To the moon in 2089?" Dee quipped.

"Nowhere! Dylan's bringing over a video game, and we're going to watch him so we can learn how to play."

"Watching someone play a video game? Sounds thrilling. Not!"

"It'll be the best thing! Dylan said it has lots of cool graphics." Joey was bubbling over with excitement. "Um, Dee?"

"What? I AM TRYING TO READ!"

"They're coming..." The doorbell rang. "We need to use the TV in this room, so leave now!"

"Geez, Joey; you could ask nicely." With that, Dee got up and went to her room. She could hear the three of them laughing at something. They seemed to be having a lot of fun. Video games weren't really her go-to activity. Reading a book—now *that* was her idea of fun.

Dee hadn't thought to make her own plans. She decided to call Elena, who agreed to come over the following day. Dee wasn't sure what they would do. It was hard when inviting new people, especially when you had no clue about their interests. She felt a bit nervous and imagined sitting in boring silence, not knowing what to do.

The next day, Elena arrived with a small backpack over her shoulder. "Hi, Dee!"

"Hi! What's in the backpack?" Dee was curious. *Did she think she'd be sleeping over? Oh boy!*

"Well, I wasn't sure what you like to do, so I thought I'd bring some stuff, and between us, we could choose. You know, something from your house and something from mine."

Dee smiled. Elena was likely worried about the same thing she was worried about. "You first. What's in the backpack?"

Elena unzipped it and pulled out one item at a time. "I brought a video game in case you're into that. This one is cool. It's a racing game, so both of us could play it. I also brought some cards in case you like to play card games. And then I brought this." She hesitated before letting Dee see it. "You might not like it, but I took a couple DVDs out of the library. I haven't seen them yet."

Dee reached for them and laughed a hearty laugh when she saw one of the options. "*The Wizard of Oz* is my *favorite* movie! Shall we?"

"Sure!" Elena breathed a sigh of relief.

The movie was long, and Dee stopped it in the middle to get a snack. She returned with two glasses of lemonade and a bowl of popcorn. After the movie was over, Einstein came into the living room and jumped up onto Dee's lap.

"Dee! Your dog looks a lot like Toto!" Elena exclaimed.

"Yes, he does. Meet Einstein!"

"Hello, Einstein! I'm guessing you're a smart dog, to have such a name."

"That's right! He wouldn't let some wicked witch take him away. Would you, Einstein?"

Einstein barked spiritedly, but not at that comment. He had spotted another dog through the sliding glass door and ran for it. The glass impeded his progress, but the barking continued.

Dee and Elena got up for a closer look. The dog was

a large Doberman pinscher that should have been on a leash.

"Okay, maybe he's not *always* the smartest dog. Einstein, don't bark at dogs that are four times your size!" Dee reprimanded him. She then turned to Elena. "Let's play a game."

Dee suggested Monopoly, and while they were setting up the game, the topic of Jeremy came up.

"Elena, have boys always picked on Jeremy?"

"He wasn't in any of my classes until I was moved up, so I didn't know him. Not to be rude, but do you know what happened to his face?"

Dee sighed. "No, I don't, but no one should be mean to someone who has something like that. It must be hard to look different. And it doesn't matter, because he's really nice and funny."

"I like him, too. He's a whiz at science! I'm glad you yelled at those boys so that I could have a reason to meet you and get to know Jeremy."

Elena passed out the correct amount of money, and the game was underway. The girls appeared to be about tied in terms of properties and money when it was time to end the visit.

Elena's mother was at the door. She talked with Mrs. Lanson while the girls were cleaning up the game. Dee hoped that her mother was making a friend too.

Later that night, Dee wrote to Samantha.

Hi Samantha,

How are you? By the time you read this we'll have probably talked, and all of this will be old news. But I like to get letters in the mail, so let's keep writing!

Elena came over today, and you'll never guess what movie she brought – The Wizard of Oz! Does it make you think of anyone? LOL

What are you up to? Do you and Sue get together much? I wish we could all hang out together. Sorry I haven't been in touch much lately. Our school is on vacation this week, so I have more time.

Any more Ronnie news?

Dee

It seemed weird to Dee that she had two sets of friends in two different places. However, she was grateful that life in Florida was finally settling down. It had been a long time coming.

CHAPTER TWENTY-THREE

THE EXPERIMENT

It had been weeks since Dee heard from Samantha or Sue. She had been busy with school and her new friends, so she hadn't been good about keeping up with communication on her end.

First, there had been book reports to do in English class. Then, the science teacher invited everyone to come up with a science fair project. Dee chose to test out the effects of gibberellin on marigold plants. She was setting out to prove the claim that the plants would grow taller if given this hormone.

At home, she had set up six plastic cups for the controls—the plants that would not be treated with the hormone. Then she set up six cups for those that would receive the recommended dose. She was curious to see if that dose would prove to be better than a different one. So, she set up six more that would receive *half* the recommended dose, and another six to receive *double* the recommended dose. A large, sunny living-room window with a wide sill proved to be the ideal spot for her experiment.

Taking care of 24 plants that she raised from seeds was hard work! In the beginning, she worried that the seeds wouldn't sprout. When one of the control plants germinated first, she panicked and thought her experiment would not turn out well. But within a day or two, the others had caught up, and she relaxed.

Every other day, she took measurements of all 24 plants. After a couple of weeks, most of the ones treated with gibberellin were taller than the controls. She kept a little notebook next to the plants, in which she recorded all of her measurements. She took photos once a week.

One afternoon, she noticed that some of the control plants appeared to be taller than the treated ones. Convinced that she had made a mistake in the experiment, she rechecked her measurements and all the doses of gibberellin.

Joey dashed by her and noticed her distress. "What's wrong with you?"

"The experiment is all messed up; I must have mixed up the doses of gibberellin. Look! The tallest plants are the untreated ones. I don't get it."

Joey laughed. "Gotcha! I mixed them up last night to see if you'd notice."

"YOU DID WHAT?" Dee got up and chased after him, up the stairs to his room.

"MOM, HELP! Dee's after me!" Joey tripped and fell, giving Dee a chance to catch up.

"WHY DID YOU MESS WITH MY EXPERIMENT? IT'S FOR THE SCIENCE FAIR, YOU LOSER!"

Mrs. Lanson scrambled up the stairs to settle the dispute. "What's going on here?"

Both sides excitedly told their version of the story. Joey was reprimanded for messing with Dee's experiment and was grounded for two days. Then, Mrs. Lanson and Dee went down to the living room to try to figure out what to do.

Suddenly, Dee brightened. "I take pictures of the growth every week. I'll look at them and try to figure it out." That turned out to be an easy task because the latest photos had been taken only two days before.

Dee then labeled the bottom of each cup in permanent marker, so that there would be no mix-up in the future. Joey had gotten into mischief before, but this was over the line—*way* over.

Three days later when the grounding was lifted, Joey reserved the living room for a get-together with his friends. It seemed it would be another video-game day, so Dee made plans to see Elena. The girls decided to go play mini-golf. Dylan's mom brought him and Anika to play with Joey, and then scooped Dee for the girls' outing.

Joey was excited to have Anika and Dylan over. He had set up the video game console in hopes of having a three-way car race competition. However, Anika seemed more interested in the plants on the windowsill than the video game. She asked Joey a lot of questions, and he answered them as best he could. Dylan joined her, and they talked about plants and photosynthesis.

"I think that treatment is making these plants grow better," Dylan noted.

"Yeah, I guess so," Joey said, eager to play the car racing game. Finally, he was able to drag Dylan and Anika away to join him.

Anika got bored and left the game after losing two races. She searched through a chest of toys in a corner of the room. "Ooh, Legos are fun!" she said. There was no comment from the boys.

Next, she found a lightweight foam football and baseball. Both had a squishy feel to them, and she liked to squeeze them. "Do you want to play catch?" Still no comment. She threw the football at Joey, and it hit him gently off the head.

"Hey!" he said, getting up. Dylan followed, and they tossed the ball back and forth. Joey bragged that he could throw the football like an NFL quarterback. He threw it hard to Anika, and it bounced off her outstretched arms and landed on top of some of Dee's plants!

"Uh-oh!" Joey ran to the windowsill and saw that the ball had flattened some of the plants and knocked others over, spilling the dirt from the cups. He tried to prop up the bent-over ones, but nothing worked.

"Get some straws or sticks, and we can tie the plants to them so they'll stand up," Dylan suggested. Joey found some straws and twist-ties and splinted the plants so they would look tall once again.

Anika helped to replace the soil in the ones that had tipped over.

* * *

Dee had played mini-golf only once before, at a birthday party for a classmate. This mini-golf place had many fun and challenging holes.

Elena got a hole-in-one on her third hole, and Dee cheered loudly, even though she herself was not doing as well. The score was pretty close by the end, but Elena had her beat by three strokes.

In the middle of the second round, Dee began to feel faint. It was sunny, hot, and humid—the perfect recipe for trouble, in her experience. She started requiring five strokes for every hole and seemed to lose interest in the game.

"Are you all right, Dee?" Elena's mother asked. "You look pale."

"I don't feel well," Dee replied.

"Whoa, Dee—you're white as a ghost!" Elena noted.

Elena's mother guided Dee over to a bench and told her to put her head between her knees. She then directed Elena to sit with her, so that she herself could get Dee some water. Luckily, the concession stand was just a few yards away.

When Elena's mother returned with waters for all, Dee gulped hers as though she had been without water for a week. It was then decided that the outing was over, even though they had a few more holes to play.

Once in the car, Elena's mother passed out orange juice boxes.

"Thanks," Elena said. "My mom always brings juice boxes in the car, in case we get cranky!"

Dee was embarrassed that she had almost fainted in the heat. "I'm not used to being outside when it's so hot."

"Don't worry. We've lived here for years, and I sometimes have the same problem." Elena was sympathetic.

Soon, they pulled into the Lansons' driveway. Dee walked into the house and went straight to her room. Elena's mother came in to give an account of the episode to Mrs. Lanson. It wasn't long before there was a knock on Dee's door.

"Are you okay?" Her mother sounded concerned.

"Yeah, I am now. But it's so hot here! I can't get used to it." Dee's tone was desperate and pleading.

"We'll have to do things differently than we're used to, especially with summer coming. From now on, we'll bring water and juice with us when we go out."

"Elena's mother does that. She gave me water and orange juice, and I did feel better. I'm okay now."

Joey was uncharacteristically quiet during supper and went to his room after the meal was done. Dee went to check on her plants, and when she saw them, she nearly fainted for the second time that day.

"MOM!!!"

* * *

Luckily for Dee, the plants were not permanently damaged. After a day or two, they appeared almost completely recovered.

Dee was hoping that Joey would be grounded for the rest of his life, but he received no punishment. He was, instead, praised for his quick action of splinting the bent-over plants, which had saved them.

"Mom, why didn't you punish Joey for wrecking my science project?" Dee asked with a bit of an edge to her voice.

"He didn't do anything intentionally. Perhaps he and his friends shouldn't have been playing with the ball around the plants, but the foam balls are light and perfectly acceptable to be tossed inside. It was an accident."

Dee decided not to argue the point, even though she didn't completely agree with it. In any case, the plants had survived, and no one would be the wiser at the science fair. She continued taking measurements and treating the plants with some or no gibberellin, as appropriate.

The presentations were coming up soon. Dee was working on her report when the phone rang.

"Sue!" she exclaimed into the phone. "I am so happy to hear from you!"

"Samantha's on the other phone, so we can all talk."

"Hi, Dee. What's new?" Samantha asked.

Dee told all her news: her two new friends, her science fair project, and her continuous struggle with the heat. "What's new with you two?"

Samantha spoke first. "My grades are still good. Penny has been a big help, especially with math. I'm back to swimming, which is awesome! One day, I want to be a life-guard." She was a skilled swimmer, so Dee was happy to hear this bit of news.

"I beat a tricky boss in my video game. I've been try-ing to beat that boss for weeks!" Sue was a video-game fanatic.

"That's great! Congrats! Any Ronnie news?" Dee inquired.

"She's about the same," Sue began. "She doesn't really talk to either of us. She's doing all sorts of weird stuff to her hair. This week, it was orange on the ends."

Samantha laughed. "Yeah, she looks strange. She's also wearing makeup now!"

"Well, maybe she's trying to impress the boys," Dee guessed.

"There are always a lot of boys around her!" Sue laughed.

"I think she looks ridiculous!"

"Speaking of ridiculous, is there any Andrew news?" *Why am I asking about him?* Dee wondered.

"He's as weird as ever," Sue offered.

"Is he still teasing everyone in sight?" Dee asked.

"Not that I've noticed," Samantha responded. "Maybe he learned his lesson after bugging you so much."

"Or he saved his teasing just for you, Dee," Sue suggested.

"I have a great idea! Why don't we put Ronnie and Andrew in the same room and see what happens?" But as soon as Dee said it, she decided it would be a *bad* idea; Ronnie might decide to go after him. *And why should I care?*

"Oh, he wouldn't be old enough for her. She likes the seventh- and eighth-graders," Sue commented.

Dee heard voices from the hall. "Sorry, but I've got to go. Let's talk again soon. Bye."

"Bye," Samantha and Sue chorused.

Dee returned to her report. After she was finished, she walked into the living room and saw Joey sitting alone. "Jerk," she said under her breath.

"Hey, I heard that! Be nice! Are you ever going to talk to me again?"

"No, I won't ever talk to you again. You wrecked my project, and no one punished you for it."

"I didn't wreck your project because I *fixed* it, after the ball landed on it. Mom said if I didn't tie the plants to the straws, they might've broken or even died. So, I'm a hero."

"Some hero. You shouldn't have been playing catch in the living room anyway."

"What do you mean? We always do! You do it, too."

"NOT AROUND A DELICATE SCIENCE FAIR PROJECT!"

"Uh, Dee... guess what? You're talking to me!" Joey gave Dee a funny smirk.

With that, Dee spun around and stormed out of the living room. She gathered up her homework and laid out her clothes for the next day. Then, for the rest of the evening, she went to any room where Joey wasn't.

CHAPTER TWENTY–FOUR

JUDGMENT DAY

The science fair came upon her fast. Her experiment had proven to be a success. The plants treated with the recommended dose of gibberellin had grown the best and looked the healthiest. The ones with a half-dose had grown taller than the controls, but not as tall as those treated with the recommended dose. The ones treated with a double dose of the hormone had grown tall, but were not healthy-looking. She had made a graph of her results, which she displayed on a poster with other visuals to enhance her project.

Students presented to the class for practice, and then would present to a judge the next day. Dee felt confident in her presentation to the class. Everyone cheered when she was finished, especially Elena and Jeremy. She returned the favor after each of their presentations.

"Well, tomorrow is judgment day," Jeremy said after class.

"I'm nervous to present to the judge. The judges are the other science teachers, you know." Dee sighed.

"Most of them are really nice," Elena offered.

"Except for Mr. Dolan. He's kind of mean," Jeremy said.

"Not exactly *mean*. I'd say more like strict and serious," Elena corrected.

"Well, I hope I get a nice judge," Dee said. "We'd better get to class, or we'll all be late! Bye, Jeremy! See you tomorrow!"

"Yeah, see ya!" he replied, and sprinted away.

* * *

The next day, the science students set up their displays in one of the gymnasiums and waited for a judge to approach and listen to their presentations. Dee could feel butterflies dancing in her stomach. She had worked hard on her project. There was no reason for her to be nervous, but she couldn't seem to help it.

Looking across the room, she noticed that Jeremy's judge was the dreaded Mr. Dolan. She felt sorry for her friend. However, his project was amazing, so he would likely do well no matter who came to judge. He had made a talking robot out of building toys that moved on battery power. It was able to "talk" by means of a small device hidden in its head. The voice was Jeremy's, but still, it was impressive. Mr. Dolan seemed to be asking a lot of questions, yet Jeremy appeared to be unfazed.

Elena was presenting to a female judge, who seemed to be very pleasant and enthusiastic. Elena's project was about seeing if she could train her pet gerbil to find food at the end of a complicated maze. Dee noticed the teacher's frequent smiles, which she hoped meant that Elena was doing well.

"Delores?" Breaking her concentration was none other than Mr. Dolan. "My, you have many plants here! Please tell me about your project."

He doesn't seem mean. Dee felt a tiny bit encouraged by that.

She told him her guess as to how the experiment would turn out. She then described the actual experiment and revealed which plants were treated with the hormone and how much, as well as which were the untreated or control plants. Finally, she concluded her presentation by explaining her graphs. When she was finished speaking, she felt relieved.

Then came his rapid-fire questions. "How did you decide which concentrations to use? What measuring tools did you use? How can you be sure the plants received equal amounts of sunlight? Do you think plants could grow without light? Or, without water?"

Dee answered everything to the best of her ability. Then came the dreaded questions. "What happened here? There appears to be some sort of injury to these plants. Did the hormone cause this?"

Wait until I get home! I'm going to tell Mom that Joey did wreck my project. She'll have to punish him then!

"Delores? I asked you a question."

Dee sighed. "My brother threw a ball, which landed on some of my plants. He tried to fix the damaged ones by tying them to straws. So, no, the hormone didn't cause this; my brother did." She avoided eye contact with Mr. Dolan.

"Do you think the hormone helped or hurt the healing process? Can you tell by looking at the plants? What is your best guess?"

Too many questions! Dee was feeling overwhelmed—and a little picked on, if the truth be told. "Maybe, because the hormone makes the plants grow, it might be able to make healing go faster." *Lame! How am I supposed to know?*

"Thank you for sharing your project with me." Mr. Dolan shook her hand. "It is obvious that you worked hard on your experiment. Good job."

Well, she had done her best. If Joey had messed it up for her, she would get him back.

At 7:30 that evening, the students and their families would return, and the winners would be announced. Dee didn't want Joey to come, but her parents insisted that he should not and would not be excluded. *Drat!*

The Lansons walked into the gym and found themselves in a crowd of excited students and their families. Dee found her project and was delighted to see a blue ribbon pinned to her poster. A red ribbon was given to those in the middle group, while a white ribbon was given to those in the lowest group; a blue ribbon meant that she had made it to the top group and was eligible for one of the three special prizes. Her parents hugged her and congratulated her.

"Hey, Dee, you can't be mad at me!" Joey beamed. "You got a blue ribbon! Will you talk to me now?"

Dee was happy with her blue ribbon and decided that she should give Joey the benefit of the doubt. "I guess so, but please don't wreck any more of my stuff." She even managed a small smile and messed up his hair, just a little.

Suddenly, Elena and Jeremy approached. "Yay! We all got blue ribbons!" Elena exclaimed. Jeremy, on the other hand, stood awkwardly by her side.

"You must be Jeremy," Mrs. Lanson said.

"Yes," he answered, avoiding eye contact with her.

Mr. Lanson smiled at Jeremy. "I would like to see the robot you built, if I may."

"Sure," Jeremy replied. They left together, with Elena and the rest of the Lanson family following close behind.

The Lansons met Elena's and Jeremy's parents. Everyone got along really well. Their conversations were interrupted by an announcement.

"May I have your attention, please?" Mr. Dolan spoke into a microphone. "I'd like to thank all the students who entered this science fair. Everyone did an amazing job. Lots of hard work went into each and every project, and you should all be proud." The room erupted in loud cheering for the students. "There were three projects in each grade that deserve special recognition, and each of these students will be awarded a special prize."

Mr. Dolan began with the eighth grade, then seventh, and lastly the sixth grade. The three families were still together as the prizes were announced. Dee, Jeremy, and Elena all had their fingers crossed.

"For our sixth-graders, the third-prize winner is Salina Mendez for her project on Paper Chromatography." The crowd cheered while Salina received her bronze medal. "Second prize goes to Valeria Costa for her project on How Music Affects Memory." There were more cheers as Valeria received her silver medal. "And, finally, first prize goes to... Jeremy Martin for his project on Robots."

Dee and Elena screamed and cheered for their friend

while he received his gold medal. Loud cheers filled the gym. Grown-ups were shaking his hand, and groups of people came to check out the award-winning project.

This time, Dee was not jealous as she used to be when everyone flocked around Pete. She was so happy for Jeremy. He was smart and really deserved all the positive attention.

Suddenly, out of the corner of her eye, she saw two of the mean boys approaching Jeremy. His parents were with Elena's parents, looking at her project. Dee held her breath.

"Congrats, bea—I mean Jeremy," the first boy said.

Jeremy looked startled as he waited for the insult that was likely to follow.

"Seriously—nice job, man," said the other. "Yours was the coolest project here. Your talking robot is awesome."

Jeremy couldn't help but smile with relief.

Dee wasn't upset that she didn't win a prize. Her blue ribbon had put her in the top group, and that was enough to make her happy. The night had gone wonderfully well, in her opinion. In fact, she couldn't have imagined a better outcome.

CHAPTER TWENTY-FIVE

SUMMER PLAN TROUBLE

The following day, Dee called Samantha. Sue was, coincidentally, visiting her. Dee told them about the science fair and Jeremy's winning the gold medal.

"That's great!" Samantha said.

"Did you win anything?" Sue inquired.

"Elena, Jeremy, and I all got blue ribbons, but only Jeremy won a prize. What's new with you guys?"

"We're glad you asked!" they chorused.

"My mom said that I can come visit you when school gets out for the summer." Samantha paused.

"And, if your parents agree, my mom said I could come, too!" exclaimed Sue.

"AWESOME!" Dee thought the news was the best she had ever heard. "I'll check with Mom about it, but I'm sure she'll say yes. This will be the best summer ever!"

"What're you so happy about?" Joey asked when Dee got off the phone. "Maybe you're happy that your new boyfriend won the science fair?"

"Jeremy is not my boyfriend!" Dee threw a pillow at Joey and chased him up the stairs. *Why do boys have to tease everyone?* Then, a terrifying thought occurred to her. *What if Joey grows up to be like Andrew and annoys everyone in sight? Or just me?*

Dee ran back down the stairs to ask her mother about the summer. "May Sue and Samantha come to visit me this summer? Please?"

"Both together, or separately?" Mrs. Lanson wanted to hear all the facts before giving an answer.

"Together, I think. That's what it sounded like to me. Please, Mom?"

"How long will they stay?"

"I forgot to ask. All summer?" Dee pleaded.

"Well, Dee, that's a lot to ask. Having two more people in the house all summer would be very challenging. What if Joey wanted Samuel and another friend to come? Then there would be *four* extra people."

Her mother knew Joey very well. He would insist upon that. "Will you ask Dad?"

"We will discuss it tonight. In the meantime, don't make any promises to Sue and Samantha. Three can be a challenging number. Someone might feel left out, which would make things awkward; it might be better to have one at a time. I'll see what Dad thinks, and we'll let you know."

Dee sauntered away and began trying to figure out a solution to the three-friend challenge. After Ronnie left the group, the Trendy Trio had gotten along fine, but they didn't live together 24/7. Dee didn't want anyone to feel left out.

Elena! She could be the fourth person, thus solving the problem.

Dee snuck away, taking the phone with her. Closing the door to her room, she dialed Elena's number.

"Hello?"

"Hi Elena, it's me," Dee said, barely above a whisper.

"Why are you whispering?"

"I want to ask you something, and I don't want anyone to hear."

"Okay. What's up?"

"My friends from home—my old home—want to come here for a visit this summer, but Mom said that three's a bad number. I want you to meet my friends. Would you like to be here, too, to make four?"

Elena paused, not sure what to think about this question. "Well, I was hoping that *we* could hang out this summer. But if you're going to be busy with them..."

"No, wait! I want to hang out with all of you! My friends are fun. I know you'd like them."

"So, if I say yes, your friends will come for the whole summer?" There was a chilly quality to Elena's voice. "Are you asking me only because you won't be able to see your friends if I say no?"

This conversation was not going well. "Elena, you are my best Florida friend! I want you to meet my friends from my old hometown. I like all of you, and I think it would be fun to spend the summer together. Maybe we could all sleep in the living room."

"I'll think about it. Wait, so I'd sleep over? All summer?"

"Why not? It'll be like sleepaway camp at my house!"

"It could be fun." Elena seemed to be warming up to the idea. "Let me know."

Just then, Joey came bounding into the room. "I want to have *my* friends over this summer. You can't be a hog! I heard you making plans to have friends here all summer. I'm telling Mom!"

"I have to go. See you tomorrow." Dee hung up the phone. "Joey, were you listening to my private conversation? You can't do that!"

"Well, I did hear it."

"How? Were you outside the door?"

"This Sherlock Holmes will never reveal his methods."

Dee was furious. "Mom!"

* * *

That evening after supper, the parents got together to discuss options for the summer. Joey and Dee had given Mrs. Lanson an earful after she broke up their fight.

The family was called together for a meeting. Mrs. Lanson spoke first, to Dee. "It is unfortunate that you spoke to Elena before we made our decision. Dee, I asked you not to do this. Our house is not big enough to accommodate three or four more people living with us. Now you will have to undo what you have done."

Dee was guilty as charged and would have to fix the mess she had made. Crossing her fingers, she waited for the final decision.

Mr. Lanson spoke next. "We feel the summer should be split up so that there will be only one guest here at a time. Dee, you can have a friend over for the first and third weeks of July. Joey can have a friend here for the second and fourth weeks. How does that sound?"

Dee was disappointed, but she knew that it would be

useless to argue the point. "Our old school gets out later than our new school. Could we have Elena and Dylan over while we wait for the other school to let out?"

Joey's eyes brightened. "You mean, for a sleepover?"

The parents looked at each other, remembering the last sleepover that included both sets of friends. Not a good scene! "Yes, you may have your friends sleep over, but on different nights." Mrs. Lanson was quite firm on this point. "We'll make out a schedule to help us keep the peace," she added.

Dee and Joey could feel their mother's gaze upon them: first to one, and then to the other.

Mr. Lanson took out a calendar and penciled in the dates that were approved for friends. Dee was disappointed that she wouldn't be having all of her friends around her all summer, but she'd take what she could get.

Once in her room, she lay on her bed and tried to imagine what the summer would be like. Suddenly, she had an idea. *I'll keep a diary! I'll write down everything we do!* She couldn't wait for the school year to end so that she could see her old friends!

* * *

Finally, it was the last day of school. Dee had spent less than half a year in her new school. The time had breezed by, and she was proud of herself for adjusting so well.

Elena and Jeremy had filled the friendship void very nicely. In fact, they had all become the best of friends. Dee ended the year with mostly A's on her report card, which made her feel proud. On the flip side, the intensity of the Florida heat had not been easy for her to cope with, but she had found a way to survive it. However, the hottest days were yet to come.

At lunch, Dee and Elena were making plans for their five-day "sleepover camp" at Dee's house, beginning that afternoon. Jeremy was especially quiet, which Dee noticed and tried to ease. "Jeremy, are you going away soon?"

"Nope."

"Well, Elena and I are taking a 'vacation' at my house! It would be fun to have you over sometimes, too, if you'd like to join us."

"I don't think my parents would let me sleep over," Jeremy said.

Dee was stunned. "Jeremy, not to sleep over but to *visit*!" She bopped him on the arm.

He smiled. "I was just trying to bug you! I knew what you meant."

"Well, don't bug me. I had enough of that from..."

"Andrew," Jeremy interrupted. "I know all about Andrew."

Dee felt totally embarrassed. "Will you come over if we call you?"

"Sure. It'd be fun. Thanks."

When the bell rang at the end of the day, the students erupted in a loud, boisterous cheer. "Summer's here! Yahoo!" It became a chant, repeated over and over until the last bus pulled away.

Upon arriving home, Dee scrambled to find the new diary she had bought, but it was not where she had left it. The location of her missing diary could be explained in only one word. *Joey.*

She entered his room, which was a mess of astronomical proportions. Normally, bedrooms were not to be entered without permission, but Joey wouldn't be home for another half-hour or so. Also, this certainly qualified as an emergency.

She looked through the piles on the floor—no luck. His desk was piled high with all kinds of things. She tried to look without disrupting the piles, but all of a sudden, one tall pile went sliding off the desk and onto the floor. *Oops!* No diary there, either. She tried to reassemble the mess the way it was, but she had forgotten how it initially looked. *My bad.*

She left no stone unturned, so to speak, and was no closer to finding the diary. *I know.* Sliding her hand under his mattress, she felt a book and pulled it out. *Eureka!*

"WHAT ARE YOU DOING IN MY ROOM?" Joey screamed from the doorway.

"Looking for this!" Dee held up the diary—except it wasn't her diary! She turned over the book, which was the size and shape of her diary, and saw that it was on video-game cheat tactics and how to beat your opponent.

"Hey, give me that!" Joey snatched it out of her hands. "How did you know about this?"

Thinking fast, Dee said, "Now we know why you always win. I'm going to tell everyone you're a cheat."

"But I'm not! I haven't even read it yet! A kid at school gave it to me yesterday, and I never even opened it."

"But you were *going* to!"

"Well, I'm telling Mom that you were snooping in my room," Joey retorted.

"Let's make a deal. I won't tell anyone about this, if you won't tell Mom or Dad."

"Deal."

That solved one problem, but the missing diary was another. Where could it be?

As it turned out, the diary had fallen beneath the table in the living room where Dee had originally placed it. She shouldn't have worried about Joey finding it; after all, it was blank. She couldn't wait for the summer to begin!

CHAPTER TWENTY–SIX

DEAR DIARY

Summer had come and was nearly over now. How quickly it was passing!

The day was hot and humid, and Dee decided to stay inside. After pouring herself some lemonade, she picked up her diary to reminisce about the fun she had had with her friends. She opened the diary to the first page and began reading.

Elena's Sleepover

Wow, school is over and I'm happy. I escaped being beaten up by those mean boys! Got caught looking in Joey's room for you, dear diary! Glad I found you. Elena and I are doing sleepover camp here. How weird is that?! We stayed up almost all night. I'm writing this by flashlight. She's asleep. And snoring. Sigh...

Whoops! I forgot to write for a couple days.

Elena and I went to the beach with Mom. It's SO hot here! I dream of snow! We then came home and watched *Ice Age* movies. We watched all of them in two days! Joey kept bothering us, though. Why do people have to put up with annoying little brothers?

Mom took us shopping and out for ice cream. No annoying boys like Andrew there!

Hello again, diary! Jeremy just left. We had fun! We played word games and watched an old *Spiderman* movie. Elena is in love with Spiderman, I think! She went on and on about how cute he was. Then we played one of Joey's racing games. Yes, I played a video game! Gasp! Jeremy won. I wonder if he read Joey's cheat book!

The last day of our sleepover camp was rainy, that walk-outside-and-drown-yourself type of rain. Ugh! We stayed inside, and it was boring. Joey was stuck inside, too. He invited us to play time machine with him. Trust me, I wanted to send him back to the beginning of time and leave him there. No, actually, we had fun with him. (Don't tell anyone.) We zipped back to dinosaur days and pretended that Joey was eaten by a T-Rex. Then, we leaped to 1969 and all walked on the moon. That part wasn't boring.

Elena is my new best friend! Bye for now!

Dylan's Sleepover

Every time I want to go into a room, the

boys are in there. Annoying! But Joey's having fun, and Dylan's a nice kid. Not annoying like SOME boys. They play video games and yell and cheer a lot. Not good when I'm trying to read! Mom took them out sometimes. Then it was quiet!

I called Sue and Samantha. I can't wait for their visits. Wish we could all be together, but Mom and Dad said no. Yes, dear diary, I'm pouting at that! Just a few more days...

Sue's Sleepover

Sue came for her sleepover camp. She looks a little different—taller than when I saw her last. I wonder if I look different to her. We talked for hours and hours! It was fun hearing all the news from home, but a little sad too. I miss home. Ronnie was still ignoring everyone, but Sue said she looked unhappy on the last day of school. No one had seen Pete. Drat! I wanted Pete news! No Andrew news either. Yay!

Yikes! I forgot to write again. Sue and I are having a lot of fun. Yesterday, she whomped me at Monopoly. Ouch!

Today, Sue met Elena! We all went over to Elena's house for a cookout. We played volleyball, and Joey and Dylan were SO into it! Sue tripped over the net support and cut her knee on a rock. Luckily, she didn't need stitches, just a big bandage. That ended the game for us. At night, we all went to see the fireworks. That was awesome! Sue and Elena seemed to like each other.

Sue left, and I am sad. ☹

Samuel's Sleepover

Somebody, rescue me! Joey is over-the-top excited these days. I guess he had been missing his friends from home. They're up late and making noise every night. Dear diary, I need earplugs!

Samantha's Sleepover

Samantha looks different, too! I felt like I hadn't seen her for years, not months. We talked and talked and talked some more! Penny has done wonders for Samantha's confidence. She's so happy now! She ran into Ronnie at the mall, and Ronnie pretended not to see her, even though they were walking right toward each other! What's up with that? Samantha also brought Pete up; yes, she brought him up, diary! I think she likes him, too. No surprise there! He's cute!

Oops! I forgot to write again! Samantha, Mom, Joey, and I had a nice day at the beach, except for the feeling-sick-after-a-day-in-the-sun problem. Have I mentioned, dear diary, that I hate the heat?

We went shopping and to the movies, watched videos, and talked more! Elena came over to meet Samantha, and we had fun! I'm glad my friends like each other.

Dear Diary, I am very sad. ☹ *Samantha left today, and we both cried. We cried, diary! I miss my friends! Why can't I have everyone in one place?*

Surprise Visit

While Joey had another friend from home over, I got a surprise. Penny came to visit me! She was here visiting her cousin Anika. She told me that Samantha was very sad to leave me, and I almost cried again. Penny is nice. She brought me some books to read. I love to read! She knew just what would cheer me up.

Well, diary, July was fun. I have only two more weeks off before school starts again...

That was the last entry Dee had written. *Wait a minute! What's this?* There was writing on the right-hand page.

Dear Diary,

I love boys. Boys, boys, boys! Jeremy, Pete, Andrew, Spiderman, but everyone knows the best boy in the world is my excellent brother Joey. He's the most awesome time-traveler there ever was.

"Joey, I'm going to get you for this!" Dee ran out of the room, found him, and chased him across the kitchen floor. "Stay out of my stuff!"

"Back at ya! You went into my room without permission. Revenge is sweet!" He dodged out of her way, just barely escaping her reach.

Mrs. Lanson stopped them when they reached the living room. She waited for the mutual tattling session, but there wasn't one. Maybe they were finally able to settle some of their own disputes. Once she was convinced that things were settled, at least for now, she went outside to get the mail. When she returned, she had an odd-looking envelope and handed it to Dee.

"For me?" Dee looked at the envelope and saw her name on it. There was no return address. She hoped it was a letter from one of her friends from home.

When she opened it, a pen and small pad of paper fell out. The top sheet said:

DEE'S PEOPLE I MISS LIST

ANDREW

Dee turned the page, but it was blank. She recognized the writing. It was, indeed, Andrew's.

Putting down the notepad, she twirled the pencil between her fingers. *How did he know my address? Sue and Samantha wouldn't have told him, would they? What does this mailing mean?* Dee couldn't imagine. She was speechless.

Should I write and ask him why he did this? She thought about it for a long while but decided to let it go for now. What did anything about Andrew matter? Her life was here—in the middle of a heat wave—with different friends in a land that was once foreign to her. Yet, she had settled in somehow. Apparently, miracles do happen.

Retreating to her room, she lay on her bed. She was

amazed at how life had unfolded. Thinking about how she faked heat sickness when the family first visited Florida made her smile. If they had stayed in New England, she never would have met her new friends. Elena and Jeremy were awesome!

She also found herself thinking about Joey's time-machine obsession. If she could go back in time—to a time before the move—would she choose to do it? When she thought about Elena and Jeremy, she suddenly felt unsure. *Why can't I have the best of both worlds? That is exactly what I plan to do!*

In the end, she decided that change could be good and might bring on new and exciting adventures. Suddenly, she wasn't afraid of change; she would look ahead without fear. *New experiences? Bring them on!*

ABOUT ATMOSPHERE PRESS

Founded in 2015, Atmosphere Press was built on the principles of Honesty, Transparency, Professionalism, Kindness, and Making Your Book Awesome. As an ethical and author-friendly hybrid press, we stay true to that founding mission today.

If you're a reader, enter our giveaway for a free book here:

SCAN TO ENTER
BOOK GIVEAWAY

If you're a writer, submit your manuscript for consideration here:

SCAN TO SUBMIT
MANUSCRIPT

And always feel free to visit Atmosphere Press and our authors online at atmospherepress.com. See you there soon!

ABOUT THE AUTHOR

Janice Laakko has many and varied interests. She enjoys different types of music. One might find her playing a guitar or positioned behind a camera!

Photography has been an ongoing interest since she was a child. She especially loves to photograph lovely scenes in nature. However, if a silly moment presents itself, it just might be preserved in a photo! *Click! Click!*

She invites you to check out her website:
https://janicelaakkoauthor.com